Praise for Avotcja's |

MW00770334

"Avotcja takes her readers on a F
picting life in the abstract as one (
this side of heaven! My favorite is

- Janie P Bess, Author "Visions"
- Founder/Director: Writers Resource Center, Fairfield, CA

"Watch out! Whether Avotcja's fronting her take no prisoners band, Modúpue, or standing, sitting or reading alone, her words roll out like thunder, raw, fast and furious in staccato, machine gun ricocheting fashion that will leave you breathless and delirious. This sister is a word demon from the word go. She will intoxicate you with her rhythms and seize you with her passion and zest for life, people and music. You won't know what hit you but you'll know you were there."

- Genny Lim
- Award-winning San Francisco Jazz Poet & Educator

"Avotcja is a unique voice among our poets, musicians, playwrights and other creative folk today. She combines a fierce, persistent and consistent passion for justice with a beauty of words, sounds and image that can take your breath away. To put it simply, Avotcja is a national and international treasure."

- Elizabeth (Betita) Martinez, Activist, Author, Educator

"I've known Avotcja for about 5 decades and I've known her to be always writing...on the bus, down some alleyway, in theater houses, in the audience, in the middle of an event, anywhere. Only time I did not see her writing was in a classroom. She explores scenes oft visited by all but missed by most: the reader will find insights mostly to the questions she poetically poses more than the answers or prescriptions of social justice she offers, as she takes you in rhumba rhythms to the streets, the fields, the news, history and current culture. Some of her words are angrily cut, and so it should be. Yet in her anger for wrongs unredressed, her images of our human capacity to love, soaked in powerful yet touching verse emerge, like spring, and trumps them all."

- Oscar Peñaranda, Author, Educator, Storyteller

"She will mother you in Blues, shame you into your best song, deliver the medicine you need when the only open store is her next poem, keeping you alive. Avotcja has been making music and magic in the Bay Area and places beyond while generations were born, grew up, and born again to her sounds and symphonies and lullabies, and Jazz. With wide heart and ear for that word we all long for, she gives us this gift. Read and enjoy."

- Leslie Simon, Coordinator, Project SURVIVE
- Instructor, Women's Studies City College of San Francisco

'Some may know Avotcja as a radio personality. She is also a jazz percussionist with her own band, Avotcja & Modúpue, with two Bay Blues Society Hall of Fame Jazz Group of the Year Awards. I first heard Avotcja read her poetry sometime in the mid-seventies. When she reads, rhythm is key & sets her apart from other poets. Rhythm runs through her; her poetry is at home in her music: many of the original compositions of Modúpue come out of her poems. Her music is at home in her poetry: she writes many poems about music, "True Confessions of a Sound Junkie," & musicians, "Oaktown Blue," "Queen Nina (Our Light in the Tunnel)" to name a few. She uses the musical elements of repetition, (adjectival) accents, & a lot of inner rhyme & near-rhyme word play to spice her poetic language. She makes distinctions. She is very clear. As I become more familiar with her writing on the page, I am amazed at how love rises out of her anger. She is tough & she is compassionate. She writes courageously about her own struggle with MS & the system of American medicine in "This Sister Ain't Quitting!!! or Life Dodgin' The Margin of Acceptable Risk." Mostly, she speaks what she sees & she sees a lot of the disenfranchised who can't speak for themselves. Thankfully, she can & does, as in "Street Children of the Night," a poem about young children roaming the streets when she is coming home late from one of her gigs.'

- Bill Vartnaw, poet laureate of Sonoma County, 2012-13

"Avotcja is one of the most powerful poetic voices I've experienced on the spoken word circuit – a musician's poet whose voice resonates from her live performances to her printed works. She will leave an indelible impression on your mind as you read her printed poems with a thoughtful and reflective spirit that stays with you. Avotcja's masterful poetry transcends observation as an ongoing constructive campaign to inspire consciousness and wisdom. She lives what she shares and there's genuine meaning because you discover her and trust her through her art."

- Daniel Yaryan, Producer/Director: Sparring With Beatnik Ghosts & The Poetry Festival Santa Cruz 2012

Diana,
Your voice is a light in our crazy
world. Thank you for being in my life.
Love you Sis!!! Bright Monsoons
Avotcja
9/6/2013

With Every Step I Take

Avotcja

Drawings by Eliza Land Shefler

published by Taurean Horn Press
P.O. Box 526
Petaluma, CA 94953
ISBN 978-0-931552-14-4
© 2013 by Avotcja,
Artwork Copyright © 2013 by Eliza Land Shefler
All rights reserved.
No part of this book may be reproduced in any manner
or by any means, electronic or mechanical,
including photocopy, recording, or any information storage or retrieval
system, without written consent of either the
author, illustrator, or their publisher.
Printed in the United States of America

Acknowledgements

—TRUE CONFESSIONS OF A SOUND JUNKIE
(performed at AFRO SOLO @ Theater Artaud, San Francisco, CA
        8/19/99)
(On CD, "21st CENTURY MUSICISM" [Origins/True Confessions Of
A Sound Junkie] by KARLTON HESTER, HESTERIA MUSIC 2006)
—DIASPORA NEGRA/translation BLACK DIASPORA
(1st performed & written for De Rompe y Raja's Diaspora Negra
        @ La Peña Cultural Center Berkeley, CA 8/14 & 15/09)
(in *LA LUNADA, 10 Year Anthology*, San Francisco, CA 5/2010)
—GLOBAL AFRICAN JAZZ DANCE (IT'S A DJALI* THING)
written for/performed @ the Global African Jazz Fest & Symposium
        w/Randy Weston, Henri Pierre Koubaka, Hotep Idris Galet,
        Karlton Hester, etc.
at University of California/Santa Cruz & Center For African & African
        American Arts & Culture/San Francisco, CA 2003
—BIG MAMA'S MINIATURE MIRACLES
(written for/first performed @ The Watershed Environmental Poetry
Festival, Berkeley City College/Atrium, Berkeley, CA Sat 11/1/07)
(in "Sinister Wisdom 77/Environmental Issues" Berkeley, CA 2009)
(printed in Asili Press Inc., Vol VIII-3 Miami Dade, Florida 7/14/2009)
—A VERY SUBJECTIVE VIEW OF "OPERATION WETBACK"
(first appeared in "Social Justice," San Francisco, CA 1993)
(appears in "Que Odee Sola, University of IL Press," Chicago, IL)
—ANANSI THE MIRACULOUS
(written for/performed w/Diamano Coura West African Dance Co.
@ Malonga Casquelourde Center For The Arts, Oakland, CA 3/06)
—MAMA TRIED TO WARN YOU
(written for & performed w/Diamano Coura West African Dance Co.
@ Malonga Casquelourde Center For The Arts, Oakland, CA 3/06)
—THE RHYTHM IN US (DRUM CALL FOR DIAMANO COURA) 3/5/09
(written for w/Diamano Coura West African Dance Co.
& performed @ Berkeley Community Theater, Berkeley, CA 3/14/09)
(printed in Asili Press Inc. Vol VIII-3, Miami Dade, Florida 7/14/09)
—STREET CHILDREN OF THE NIGHT
(PÁ LOS CHIQUITITOS DE LA NOCHE EN QUALQUIER LUGAR)
(first printed in "Street Spirit Vol 14, No. 11, a publication of the
American Friends Service Committee Oakland, CA November 2008
—OAKTOWN BLUE
Choreo/Poem/Play first performed @ Alice Art Center, Oakland, CA
        6/1/2002
performed @ James Moore Theater, Oakland, CA 2/2003
performed @ Art & Soul Literary Stage, Oakland, CA 8/2004
(on CD, "Live @ Yoshi's" by Avotcja & Modupue,

World Of Wordpower & Song, 2004)
(on CD, "Bridge Across The Blue" by Avotcja & Modupue & misc.
Artists, Word & Violin, 2004)
—KUDUL KHELATE/THE UNCONCIOUS
(written for "Reflections" & performed w/Diamano Coura West
African Dance Co. @ Malonga Casquelourde Center For The Arts,
Oakland, CA 3/ 9 & 10/07)
—COSMIC SOUL MATES
(performed/videotaped at SF State World Music and Dance Event,
honoring the memory of esteemed Dance faculty member Alicia
Pierce) @ Knuth Hall, San Francisco State University, SF 4/29/2009
(in *The Journal Of Pan African Studies*, Vol. 4, #2, Poetry Issue,
        Guest Editor MarvinX, Phoenix, AZ 12/10)
—THE TRUE QUEEN OF CARNIVAL
(A TRIBUTE TO CONNIE WILLIAMS)
(first printed in "The Caribbean," Oakland, CA 10/92)
(in "Black Culture Magazine," Vacaville, CA 1993 & 1994)
—THERE'S SOMETHING MISSING
or AIDS: THE THIEF THAT MAKES OUR ANCESTORS CRY
(featured in "AFRO SOLO!" Western Addition Cultural Center, San
        Francisco, CA 2000)
—IN THE NIGHT (WHEN ALL YOU CAN SAY IS MMMMM!!!)
(on CD, "Live @ Yoshi's" by Avotcja & Modupue,
        World Of Wordpower & Song, 2004)
—MEMORIES IN THE MANY KEYS OF HORIUCHI
(on CD, "Live @ Yoshi's" by Avotcja & Modupue,
        World Of Wordpower & Song, 2004)
—LA REGLA DE LOS LADRONES/THE DIVINE LAW OF THIEVES
(in *El Tecalote*'s 40th Anniversary Issue, San Francisco, CA 8/2010)
—OMBLIGAO EN ARGENTINA (RECORDANDO LA MAJESTAD DEL
TANGO)/translation NAVEL TO NAVEL IN ARGENTINA (REMEMBER-
ING THE MAJESTY OF TANGO)
(Recorded by Avotcja w/ The Musical Art Quintet on the CD, *Nuevo
Chamber Classical,* Revolution Records, San Francisco 2012)
—IT AIN'T EASY
(performed in "Conceptions" by Purple Moon Dance Project,
        SomArts Theatre, 6/1999)
—LISTEN TO THE RAIN
(on audio cassette "Has Anybody Heard My Song???" by Avotcja,
        1989)
(performed as part of "Avotcja's Song,"
AFRO SOLO @ ODC Theater, San Francisco, CA 8/27/94)
—ROBLESQUE (TO AL ROBLES WITH LOVE)
(performed/videotaped at Tribute to Al Robles
        @ Ninja's San Francisco, CA 6/27/09)

(performed/videotaped at Al Robles Memorial
            @ Glide Memorial Church, San Francisco, CA 7/25/09)
—TIME IS A HEARTLESS BABYSITTER
(in *Out Of Our # 4*, Fall 2009, S.F., CA 10/14/09)
(printed on Poets Respond To SB1070/Facebook/Avotcja 7/2/10)
—LOVE SONG FOR A LOVABLE PEOPLE
(on audio cassette "Has Anybody Heard My Song???" by Avotcja,
            1989)
—ANCESTRAL REFLECTIONS
(written for "Reflections" & performed w/Diamano Coura West
African Dance Co. @ Malonga Casquelourde Center For The Arts
Oakland, CA 3/ 9 & 10/2007)

WITH EVERY STEP I TAKE
(SHORT STORIES & POETRY)
by AVOTCJA
with ARTWORK BY
ELIZA LAND SHEFLER

This miracle that you hold in your hands would have never been possible without the unfailing encouragement & kind support of The California Arts Council, Zellerbach Family Fund, Afro Arts, The East, Women of Color Resource Center, Serpent Source Foundation For Women In the Arts, The Blues Foundation, Thomas Simpson & Afro Solo, Writers Resource Center, La Peña Cultural Center, Jazz In Flight, The Pat Bond Award, The Mission Cultural Center for Latino Arts, Ustadi Kaderi & Robert Woods of The African Childrens Advanced Learning Center, Kim McMillan, Al Young, & Ishmael Reed of PEN Oakland, The Bay Area Blues Society, and last, but definitely not least, Q.R. Hand & Bill Vartnaw & Taurean Horn Press Books who believed in my dream and helped me bring it to life. ¡Ashé! I thank you all!

Table Of Contents

ARTWORK
by Eliza Land Shefler

I am an artist, poet, singer/songwriter, and pianist, constantly seeking new ways to combine the arts. I came to the Bay Area to go to California College of Arts & Crafts, where I wrote, illustrated, hand-set, printed and hand-bound 2 books of poetry, as well as creating a hand-drawn animation. Soon after I moved to Oakland, I was captivated by all the wonderful jazz music I heard around the Bay, and I began playing jazz in the 1980's, performing at clubs and restaurants throughout the Bay Area. From January 2001- September 2009, I co-hosted Rhythm & Muse, an open mic series for spoken word and music. I met Avotcja in the late '80's, when I was seeking poets and musicians for a jazz and poetry concert at Kimball's for the Bay Area Jazz Society, later to become Jazz in Flight. (I'm a founding member of both organizations.) When I first heard Avotcja perform, I felt that I'd met the right person to bring to life my dream of music and poetry making magic together; I was very honored when she asked me to illustrate this book.

ON "WITH EVERY STEP I TAKE"

Reading Avotcja's work takes me back in time. It takes me back to the sound of Afro-Latin drums in Sproul Plaza at U.C. Berkeley, to street corner sweet talk in "The Mission" in San Francisco, to the rumbling forests of Puerto Rico, to death defying demonstrations in the streets, to struggles for African and All People's Liberation.

We could call this a book of poems, of pictures, of politics and pain and it is all that...but more it is a record of collective memories. As the music of her words dance between these pages we are carried along the current of our history. The words here record a history of leontine courage. The courage to love in spite of cruelty, to fly in the face of death, the courage to challenge "Stereotypes & Thangs".

We could call this a book of love poems. For certainly there is deep longing, delicate loving and losing familiar to us all in these poems & these stories.

There are songs to the Earth here. In "Yemayalandia"...
"The creatures of darkness dance and sing
When night falls at the bottom of the Sea"
We are serenaded on bright Summer days in Harlem, and seduced by rainy autumn nights by the Bay. The Folk Story "Free Like The Birds" achieves justice through mystery, and a walk in the park will never be the same for certain people.

Throughout this work, respect and recognition are given to the creative contributions of artists (some are Ancestors now) who have sung us to sleep, drummed us awake, and kept us alive in the madness.

Avotcja is a Mother, Lover, Warrior, and a Muse. She has chronicled our journey in Spanish and in English, in soft whispers and deafening screams, in subtle hues and in blazing color.

For me, this is a book of memories.

Luisah Teish
Writer-Performer-Ritualist
author of *Jambalaya*

With Every Step I Take flows from a proud woman, who can be soft- spoken or, at the drop of a racist hat, cop a cold attitude whenever injustice rears its ugly head. Her poetry blends the pain and sorrow, the joy and laughter, the human strengths and weaknesses of our people. It has the will and steadfast hope for better living tomorrows. It's the heartbeat of black and brown folks and the children struggling to rise above the harsh realities of violence and poverty that are so great a part of ghetto life.

And it's about sister Avotcja too, who like many have struggled out of the twilight and flown toward the sunlight of clarity. Avotcja passes on wisdoms, garnered from her own life experience. The legacy that she passes on to the children that are here now, as well as those that are yet to be born, is indeed a beautiful one.

Truly, a must reading, most especially for all the brothers. Bravo my spiritual daughter, palante siempre.

Love, your Bro, Piri Thomas
author of
Down These Mean Streets

AUTHOR'S STATEMENT

This book is dedicated to those Ancestors whose bodies cover the Oceans' floor. Those Ancestors who were tossed into unmarked graves in the U.S.A., Africa, Asia, the Caribbean, Mexico, Central & So. America. Those who lost their limbs & lives so we could live free. A sacrifice that insured our right to read & write. And all those amazing Folks who survived & worked triple time, but still found time to dance & sing & instill pride & dignity in millions of us hard-headed children just so someone like me could write Poetry & play Music.

It has taken me 40 plus years to write this book (from 1957 to 2010). These pages are filled with the blood, sweat, and tears of all who paved the way before me. Inspiration has come to me from every place I've ever been, from the sacred & serene beautiful places, all the way to the alleys of hell & back. The Music of words & sound pictures have come to me in daydreams & come through me even when I sleep. I walk in Dreamtime. Most are new & unpublished, and some are old. Some are fact, some are fiction, some are both. People are always asking me which of the characters I write about are me, and all I can say is all of them & none of them, but they've all been part of me at one time or another. I am just another teller of stories. And once a story gets started they usually take on a life of their own & I go where they want to take me. I am just a vehicle. There are stories everywhere waiting to be told, and I'm grateful to be one of the many chosen to do the job.

I have had the honor of walking life's path with some of the greatest people on the Planet, and though I'd like to thank them all space won't allow it. Still I must acknowledge some, without whom I wouldn't be me. Like my daughters Batya & Jordana, and my 4 Grandsons, 3 Great-grandsons & my Great-grand-daughter!!! My Parents, who allowed me to inherit their artistic genes & my cousin Bill. Sister Makinya Kouyate, Jose Montoya, Ustadi Kaderi, Yancie Taylor, Sylvester, Deborah Vaughan & Dimensions Dance Theater, Betita Martinez, Shukuru Copeland Sanders, Pablo Rosales, Reginald Lockett, Ramon Piñero, Nancy Hom, Al Young, Marijo, Melanie DeMore, Pat Parker, Q.R Hand, Kim McMillan, Jazz In Flight, Genny Lim, L.C. "Good Rockin" Robinson, J.C. Burris & Big Mama Thornton, Dr. Karlton Hester, Hafez Modirzadeh, Sandi Poindexter, Francis Wong, Eliza Shefler, Anthony Smith, Leslie Simon, Camincha, Ras Mo, Mamacoatl & Oba T'Shaka. Can't forget Rahsaan Roland Kirk, who taught me how to see & hear (thank you Brother Leo!) Also Thelonious Monk, Mary Lou Williams, Ahmed Abdul Malik, & Randy Weston. Sun Ra, Art Blakey & Sabu Martinez, Silvia del Villard, Leadbelly, Lord Invader, The Duke of Iron, Linda Hill, Horace Tapscott, Betty Carter, Cortijo, Calypso Rose, James

Baldwin, Arsenio Rodriguez, Jimi Hendrix, Eric Dolphy, Pedro Juan Pietri, Jackie Torrence, Max Roach, Eddie Palmieri, Cheryl Byron, Stanley Cowell, Val Serrant & Tito Puente who gave me the courage to risk everything for the love of the Arts & the strength to live with the consequences.

WITH EVERY STEP
I TAKE

WITH EVERY STEP I TAKE

My feet stand in dreams
Run circles
Around the lakes in my mind
Climb tropical hillsides
Inside forests
Hidden behind the Tenements
And dance all sweaty
A passionate urban exorcism
Wrapped in Cortijo magic
My feet swim through concrete
And drink the wind
They sing lowdown Blues tunes
And pray with Jazz bands
My feet are Poems
Every inch on my road, a Chant
A sacred inspiration, a Song
And
With every step I take
I create

TRUE CONFESSIONS OF A SOUND JUNKIE

I.......
I am.......
I am a bonafide sound junkie
Call me a child of music
I was created/born
To the tune that called...
Two very beautiful, but incompatible Dancers together
To make love ..... to make me
To the rhythmic humming of rusty bed springs
And on that night
The slippery moans & warm sweat sounds of their love dance
Became the song that is me ... The sensuous sounds of
Their love dance sang me into existence
That night didn't walk in softly
And neither did I
I came with all the fire & wild passion of a hurricane
Like a shy tornado I came
I heard Music in the rustling of newspapers in the streets
And a symphony in the sound of dripping water
Every squeaky door & leaky faucet had its song to sing
I even heard music in the dice games on the corner
I ran wild & free
Like the Doo Wops & Mambos, Kaiso, Calypso
Boleros, & Gospel, Bombas, Sambas, Blues & Jazz
Sweet uncontrollable melodies that were everywhere
Melodies that drowned the filth of city streets
But always left a place for me
In the silence between their notes,
& every time I thought I'd lose it, 'cause
The racket was more than I could stand
Spirit said ..... Listen!
Listen!!!
Listen for the rhythm
Listen...
It's there
Listen...
All around you
There's music everywhere
Listen...
Find the rhythm
Listen to the rhythm
And when you become that rhythm

You'll find that noise is only a lonely sound
Waiting
      Waiting
            Waiting for someone
Someone who does more than just hear with their ears
Spirit said.......
Listen!
Noise ain't nothing but a lonely sound
      waiting
            waiting
                impatiently waiting
                    looking for a friend
& I knew that I could be that friend
That wild & crazy friend
Who's not afraid to grab the stage & let the people know
Noise ain't nothing but a lonely sound
      waiting for a song to sing
            waiting
                Impatiently waiting
Searching for that somebody
Somebody who'd listen long enough to make her want to sing
Someone like me
Someone like you
Someone that knew
That noise ain't nothing but a sad & lonely sound
Just another naked note
      looking for some clothes

DIASPORA NEGRA

Escuchando al aviso en los vientos Africanos
Lo mas viejo de los Viejos
De mis Bisabuelos tiró nuestro idoma en las aguas
Mejor una comida pá los tiburónes en el mar
Que un juguete trivializado pá los estafadores
Marionetas en el juego de la esclavitud
En estos días
Hablo con los espíritus de mis antepasados
Y me dicen, silencio hija
Escucha el ritmo con el alma entera
Y me dicen, en este océano de la existencia
El ritmo es un salvavidas
Y escucho
Vivo escuchando a los ritmos africanos en todo
Y me encuentro, un espíritu sempiterno
Un espíritu nacido de recuerdos en los huesos
Mi herencia renacida
En cualquier País de mi Diaspora Negra
Todavia presente … este espíritu irrompible
El latido de la cultura … Siempre cuchicheo
Compartiendo regalos de secretos ancestrales
Y hablando por los pies y bailando por mi canto

BLACK DIASPORA

Listening to the warning in the African winds
The oldest of the oldest
Of my Great-Grandparents threw our language in the waters
Better a meal for the Sharks in the Sea
Than a trivialized game for the Sharks that walk the land
Pawns in the ugly game of Slavery
These days
I speak with the Spirits of those that went before me
And they tell me, be quiet child
Listen to the rhythm with your entire Soul
And they tell me, in the ocean of existence
Rhythm is a lifejacket
And I listen
I live listening to the rhythms of Africa in everything
And I find myself, an everlasting Spirit
A Spirit born of memories hidden deep in my bones
My heritage reborn
My Black Diaspora is wherever I am
Always present … this unbreakable Spirit is
The heartbeat of my culture … always whispering
Sharing secret ancestral gifts
And dancing through my Songs & speaking through my feet!

GLOBAL AFRICAN JAZZ DANCE
(IT'S A DJALI* THING)
INSPIRED BY KARLTON HESTER & DEDICATED
TO KIMAKO BARAKA, CARLOS GARNET, VAL SERRANT,
YANCIE TAYLOR, DIANE REEVES & OLIVER LAKE

I am Poetry's musical child, a born again sound freak
I have always been here & I will always be here
And this time, like all the other times, was no accident
Someone, somewhere "in the bush"
Wished me into existence
My coming was written in a field by some no writing Ancestor
An Ancestor who was always watching
And noticed every single time Ole Massa wasn't looking
And took a break from being broken
An Ancestor,
Who was brave enough & defiant enough to risk their life
And sing & dance & pray me into existence

I am the prize
The result of all their desperation, their trials & tribulations
I am the product of all those lives lived in whispers
The dreams they died for
The wish they couldn't speak of is me
A girl child called into being as much by necessity as by love
And set free by all the unseen tears
Of too many Brothers left hanging from too many trees
Too mad to be sad, the Ancestors just spit me out
And I was back in the mix
Choice??? … Hmmm!!! … I had no say
I was given a job to do & I landed on the road
Where Howling Wolf & Sun Ra crossed paths & danced

They left me in the care of
Two very flamboyant & serious Dancers
And the air I grew up in was completely saturated with
The sweaty, graceful beauty of their Art
The sexually explicit erotic power of their syncopation
The inescapable … hypnotic centuries old gyrations
A harmonic signature of long ago times … times when
The Spirit of Poetry First put its musical spell on me
Mine is a timeless Djali* destiny
And there's no way to escape it
I even bleed in A Minor & I dream in Thirteenths &

9

Long before I was born Music took control of my soul
I never needed or wanted any of those corny nursery rhymes
A rhythmic 6/8 clave, Olatunji's Yoruba chants for peace
Art Blakey's passion & Drums
Called in the supernatural voice of Sabu
It was Sabu Martinez who sang my liberation dance
And I fell asleep listening to the trees breathe
The sound of nightfall is my lullaby &
The night time is always my right time

And the complex, sensual simplicity of a Shirley Horne song
Will always make my soul sing & Big Mama Thornton???
Sister was like a triple dose of adrenaline
Cab Calloway … the spirit man of Swing
Forced me to hear with my eyes & the pure spiritual integrity
Of Mongo Santamaria left me breathless
His gift … a Latin Jazz symphony
A mystical exercise you could dance to
Left me so naturally high I had to laugh & cry
He made me wanna sing
Their Music is my medicine … a melodic phonic tonic

Jazz!!!
One of those can't live without Keys
A key that helps to set me free
Down at the Crossroads
Where it all comes together
There's a party going on & it's calling out to me
Calling my name through the Music & Poetry scene
I hear it in
The arrogantly funky wisdom of Gylan Kain & Kamau Daáood
The Avant-Garde brilliance of Jayne Cortez & Q.R. Hand
The urban dreamscapes of Sonia Sanchez & Ntozake Shange
James Baldwin's boldness
The rhythmic intensity of Margaret Walker
The out of this world worldliness of
Taalam Acey & Ishmael Reed … Their Poetry,

Another kind of Music Breathing words of fire into me
Converting negative evil speak
Into fuel for genetic mind travel
Like the Blues … one more sacred cosmic tool
A fertilizer, creating Art stronger than time
A power that makes me whole … complete … like
An Olu Dara song … Strong!!!

Brother mixes his special brand of Hoodoo
into everything that he do, his musical Storytelling
A double edged machete in times of need
Stronger than all the pain of
Chopping cane in unrelenting heat

A sanctified salve, a sweet & mellow Basie tune
A field holler … A scream
The signifying sarcasm of Barbershop Poetry
And more than once it's been my only food
When I needed something to eat
God speaks to me through this Music
It was always that special something that saved my dreams
That chased away my fears, that protected us from detection
And concealed all our schemes
It helped us grow wings called Spirituals
And we made it through … while picking fruit off trees
Listening to concerts in my head
The beautiful amazing percussion of Double Dutch memories

Salvation songs
Old familiar nameless street sounds called to me
Saved me many a day … Music … my way out of no way
The Poetry of Music, it's both my blessing & my curse
All consuming … everywhere … demanding
The Balm in my Gilead
It's alive … a Word Song … a magic … a Poem
More daring than anything Houdini ever dared to imagine
An E Major miracle … a Juke Joint jumping
Where we forgot Share Cropping, danced the nights away
'Til the sun came up on the fields the next day

Then, lo & behold I was snatched back to the Crossroads
Where the Right Reverend Charles Mingus was preachin'
Bass screamin' … sermonizing … the man was teaching
"Oh Lord
Please Don't Let Them Drop That Atomic Bomb On Me!!!"
And I testified & cried tears of joy, listening to the courage in
The magnificent voice of Carmen McRae
Singing "The Right To Love" & when Sarah Vaughan sang
Even the birds listened & I couldn't breathe
I could sense them in every breeze & almost
Feel the heat of their bodies as Katherine Dunham,
Eleo Pomare & Judith Jamison danced past
Our whirling dervishes turned life's sadness inside out

And stabilized an unstable world

While bolts of lightning flashed across the sky
Lit a fire under floors of Dancehalls gone cold
When Cubop was born
A musical earthquake shaking us awake as Dizzy Gillespie,
Chano Pozo, Mario Bauzá, Machito & Chico O'Farrill
Got together & almost Blew their brains out on a whim
Made the whole planet spin
And did a new musical balancing act
As Sonny Rollins, the Obeah Man of Bebop
Was spreading the taste of Coconut Bread everywhere
All over the place, in any land
Where there were folks who were listening to Jazz

Still greedy for more I got on board a Caribbean Cruise
And ran into Len 'Boogsie' Sharp
"Trinidad's Charlie Parker of Steel Pan"
Man was trading "Fours" with
Jon Lucien, Yusef Lateef, Shirley Scott, El Gran Fellove &
Jackeline Rago's Afro-Venezuelan Band … FIRE!
Dishing out their own special brew
A hot & spicy musical truth … It was Déjá-Vu
An original Jazzy pepper sauce, it was Quitiplas* con curry
And I still don't know if I'm following it, or it's following me

I think it's got something to do with
The rhythm of my biological clock, I mean
I can't even walk into the neighborhood Beauty Parlor, 'cause
The Drums of John Santos & Babatunde Lea are all over me
And there I am
Right back in the middle of a another Moms & Pops shop
Full of Poetry spouting Wizards & Word Conjurors
Talking smack in B Flat
Sound strong enough to wake the dead
And help the living get back on track

Knowing me, if I even tried
To close my eyes under a palm tree in Panama
I'd probably wake up to see Sandman Sims & Bunny Briggs
Tap Dancing all over Danilo Perez's Piano keys
And Eddie Jefferson working his majestic Vocalese
All over Moody's Mood For Love
The Music of his Poetry etched like stone
Deep inside the soul of me

Meanwhile, back down at that sacred place in time where
The Palladium, The Vanguard & The Sugar Shack cross paths
Ella Fitzgerald, Lady Day, Betty Carter, Dorothy Donegan,
Mary Lou Williams, Dorothy Ashby, Shirley Scott & Vi Redd
Were paving the way … cementing new ground
With the Music they played
A new kind of Sister … a master technician's technician
With all kinds of class & the sassiest sass
Worthy of a whole lot more than the dubious honor
Of being the latest showpiece on some guy's arm
These Divas ... serious
Dripping with sweat & a whole lot of
"You're gonna have to listen to me attitude!"
Jumped the fence & knocked the locks
Off the doors of the Bebop jocks & aggressively
Played their way right up to the front of the stage

There's a never ending Session
Going on down at the Crossroads
Where the living & the dead come together & Jam
John Hicks, Earl "Fatha" Hines & Don Pullen
Are always busy trading Licks & you can still find
The Blue genius of a Gene Harris groove wrapped
All the way around a Ray Brown Bass line
And get more than an earful of the elegant sophistication
Of an Ellington/Strayhorn Suite
On one of those amazing days when
The dramatically ingenious Monk refuses to play
Because some posessed Ancestral Spirit
Has pulled him off a Piano stool
And he's dancing like crazy all over the place

But not to be outdone,
I grabbed the hand of Famadou Don Moye & we ran away
With Andy & The Bey Sisters, jumped on a Melba Liston chart
And rode her Trombone all over the Motherland
Sliding down the Nile trying to catch some of
Randy Weston's African pride, while the trance like Oud
Of Ahmed Abdul Malik & Pharaoh Sanders Sax was lifting a
Veil off one more bit of the mystery of Upper & Lower Egypt
I was born a musically precocious Poetic child
I was there that day when Dinah got so Blue
Even Gregory Hines stood still & "The Sun Cried" so loud
I knew I was just about to "Drown In My Own Tears"
You can always look for me on the road

Where Cannonball & Ron Carter play
Where William Cepeda's Afro Rican Jazz crosses paths
With Omar Sosa, Cat Anderson, Sibongile Khumalo,
Dwight Trible & Hugh Masekela, all dancing
To an Etta Jones, Oscar Brown Jr., Sonny Fortune Jam,
I'll probably be finger popping
In the room in the back of Annie Mae's Cafe
Where the Musicians never stop &
John Handy & Hazel Scott, Jon Hendricks, Lorez Alexandria &
Black Arthur Blythe are throwing down &
David Murray, Eric Dolphy & James Newton are
Tearing it up on stage
Making the Ancestors smile, while Stanley Cowell is
Pulling together a new Piano Choir with Hassan,
Martha Young, Errol Garner, Horace Tapscott,
Gladys Palmer, Otis Spann, Chucho Valdes, Andrew Hill,
McCoy Tyner, Jaki Byard, Ed Kelly & Alice Coltrane

Music got so hot I tried to hide & get some rest
But along comes Edsel* with Nat King Cole & Archie Shepp
Dragging me off to yet another Gig I just can't afford to miss
Over at the Chicken Shack
"Ain't No Way" to get away when Musicians play
I just keep on coming back
I'll be somewhere backstage … listening … learning
Feeding my heart & soul
From a bowl of "Brown Rice" with Don Cherry
Hanging out with Michael White, Gatemouth Brown,
Gerald Wilson, Johnny Dyani & Charles Lloyd

Look for me … I'll be dancing
And Jamming with Jeanne Lee & Sechaba
Over at the Crossroads
Naturally high as a kite, overdosing on Vitamin B Flat
I'll be Swinging with
Nina Simone, Wayne Shorter & Jimmy Slyde
Getting down at the Crossroads
Where the living & the dead are always partying big time &
Rahsaan's still "spraying" us with his visionary soulfulness,
Electrifying & unifying the human race
Spreading his Bright Moments all over the place
And that's where I wanna be
I just got to be right there where the Music is
I won't be too hard to find
If you open your mind & listen & remember

There are too many who died to keep this magic alive
They're talking
    they're singing
        they're crying
            they're teaching
Hear their Mantra! … Are you listening???
'Cause it still "Don't Mean A Thing If Ain't Got That Swing"
And they're always
Waiting there to meet you at the Crossroads!

BIG MAMA'S MINIATURE MIRACLES

It all began with little drop of Dew
As stupidity knocked down too many trees
And the Rain ran away
When the Clouds disappeared
And arrogance lost its mind
Next some big money Jerks come pay an unasked for visit
Covered the beauty of Creation's Bounty with concrete
And a heart broken Earth turned in on her self
Brutally humiliated, the Old Girl was devastated
As she was forced to watch
Her biodiversity fade
The silent spaces where Birds used to play &
Desperate Bumble Bees, crazed Honey Bees, armies of
Disoriented Worker Bees & homeless dethroned Queen Bees
Hooked on Pollen … Starving
Slipped unnoticed into the safe obscurity of passing winds
And quietly followed the Flowers that got away
She sat,
Had to watch the Leaves fall to the ground
Feel the pain of seeing the plushest of foliage get rotten & die
Mother Nature was "pissed" & she cried
Was furious, but she just cried
She ate the hate & got sick from the steady diet of disrespect
As she tried to be "cool" & get through this re-run cycle of strife
Still under our feet all kinds of little Critters witnessed
Strawberry Creek (like the Ohlone's Mission Creek)
Being driven deeper underground looking for a safe place to hide
As sniveling greedy hypocrites worked hard at looking all-pitiful
Boo-hoo'd & tried to look like they were pushing tears aside
(In denial of their own treacherous handiwork)
Then had the nerve to curse the desiccated blandness of the Land
And the Floods of madness
That brought about the nothingness of Droughts
A souless duplication of the dryness
Of Arrogance's own lack of humanity & imagination
A continuous saga, a bankrupt drama
The arrhythmic Dance that comes from worshipping dollars
And in complete disregard of common sense
Greed wrapped itself from head to foot
Masked the sterile suicidal shame in their own self pity
And were so unbelievably busy feeling sorry for themselves
That they completely lost sight
Of the fact that they were only a small part of life

They were so self absorbed, they never even noticed
The resilient reappearance of the beauty of Clouds
Or that little ignored drop of Water
You know, the one that refused to give up the ghost
Mama's stubborn little Dewdrop
Cute little thing jumped up & gave a tiny blade of thirsty Grass
Just the right amount of courage to break through the concrete
And remind us all again, "this too shall pass"
Mama Nature has already paid the cost
And even though
She sometimes gets confused, lets go & loses control
She knows she's Mama
She knows the Earth is her home
And these days
She's spending all her time getting ready to stay ready
In anticipation of Mankind's next display of foolishness
Regardless of whether we're ready to accept the ramifications
Of humanity's actions or inaction
Mama knows … she's always known
In no uncertain terms … Earth is her Turf!!!
And it's Nature's Nature to always reclaim what's hers
Mess with just one of her Babies & even history won't miss you &
There's nothing worse than an angry Mother's fury
Nature is one of those over protective kind of Mamas that almost never plays
A Mama that will always let you know
She would much rather hold you, but if you push her too hard she'll fight
Think twice before you act unwisely
Unless you think your conscience is strong enough to handle the loss
'Cause when Nature takes, she takes it all
Big Mama's temper tantrums have been known
To turn Heaven & Hell inside out before you can blink your eyes
So while there's still a chance to do more than just think
Find what's left of common sense in your heart
Be an unwavering example of peace & harmony
Moving productively & gracefully through life like a Dewdrop
Or we're gonna lose big time … this time we're gonna lose it all
In the long run the Old Girl always wins
That's the way it's always been
That's the way the Story always goes
She's Mama … Big Mama
And Mother Nature is always Boss!

CORTE$
(CHRISTIAN SOLDIER & BRINGER OF "CIVILIZATION")

PROVERBS 15:33
The fear of God is a discipline toward wisdom, and before glory there is humility.

COLOSIANS 2:18
Let no man deprive you of the prize who takes delight in a mock humility and a form of worship of the angels, taking his stand on the things he has seen, puffed up without proper cause by his fleshly frame of mind.

PROVERBS 30:8
Untruth and the lying word put far away from me, give me neither poverty nor riches. Let me devour the food prescribed for me.

1 TIMOTHY 3:8
Ministerial servants should likewise be serious, not double-tongued, not giving themselves to a lot of wine, not greedy or dishonest gain.

EPHESIANS 5:3 & 4
Let fornication and uncleanliness of every kind or greediness not even be mentioned among you, just as it befits holy people. Neither shameful conduct nor foolish talking nor obscene jesting, things which are not becoming, but rather of giving thanks.

EXODUS 20:14 & 15
You must not commit adultery. You must not steal.

TIMOTHY 4:12
Let no man ever look down on your youth. On the contrary, become an example to the faithful ones in speaking, in conduct, in love, in faith, in chasteness.

Hernando Cortes (or Hernan Cortez depending on who's doing the writing,) a young Spanish creature in his 30's, was hand picked as the perfect man for the job of Christianizing New Spain (now known as Mexico.) According to the authorities, (most of whom were his friends,) he possessed all of the following rare qualities:

Cortes was a dreamer, arrogant, egocentric, suffered from delusions of grandeur, a religious fanatic, and a shrewd opportunist (with a sharp eye for recognizing other opportunists). He was a glutton, insanely jealous, a braggart, and a show off, an expert in divide & conquer techniques, unbelievably greedy, a condescending racist, a born gambler, an expert strategist, and extremely cruel when it benefited him. He was glory crazy, and modeled himself after that "great humanitarian" Alexander The Great*. He believed anything was condonable as long as it was done in the name of the church &

crown, and fancied himself a great lover (which was something of an embarrassment to his friends as he was known to indulge himself without restraint or regard to time or place.) He was a pathological liar & a religious hypocrite. He was also disloyal, which he proved right from the beginning, by renouncing his original intention to work for Governor Vasquez of Cuba, and going instead for personal gain & glory in his attempt to conquer Mexico.

On his arrival in Mexico he immediately indulged in blasphemy by proclaiming he was God! After defeating and calling the Indios pagans & idol worshippers, he smashed their idols and erected the usual Catholic idols in their place (the Virgin & the cross.)

To get the Spaniards off their backs, the Indios gave Cortes twenty female slaves. One of those slaves was Malintzin (she later became known by the unsavory name la Malinche,) who he gave to Puertocarrero. Although he shortly recognized in her a potentially kindred opportunistic spirit, and claimed her for himself.

"Thou shalt not covet thy neighbor's wife"

Cortes, on hearing about Tenochtitlan, was immediately interested in meeting Moctezuma (purely for reasons of conversion, of course.) And Moctezuma, on hearing about Cortes, made the mistake of trying to bribe the Spaniards to leave by sending gifts of gold, turquoise & silver. These decadent, paganistic baubles convinced Cortes that "these savages" needed Jesus more than ever! Thus, Bible in one hand (the other under la Malinche's skirts,) and weapon under his arm, he began the journey of carrying "The Word" to the very rich city of Tenochtitlan.

Moctezuma and his habit of sacrificing the members of neighboring tribes* had made him innumerable enemies. Cortes used this to his advantage and claimed to be in Mexico to bring an end to such barbarisms as human sacrifice & cannibalism. Needless to say, it was statements like this that made him thousands of friends, all of whom were enemies of Los Aztecas.

Moctezuma, on hearing that Cortes was still determined to visit him, arranged a little welcoming party for the Spaniards (made up of a couple of thousand warriors), in Cholula. After a little snooping on the part of Cortes trusty companion, interpreter, flunky & bed partner La Malinche, the Spaniards were informed of said surprise party.

Thousands of Indios were slaughtered within a few hours. The temples were burned, idols smashed, and the Cross & Virgin were erected on top of a pyramid. The remaining Indios were convinced of their burning desire to convert to Christianity. There was a mass production type baptism, mainly directed at the women (as no good Spaniard would ever sleep with a heathen.) A Mass was said in Latin,

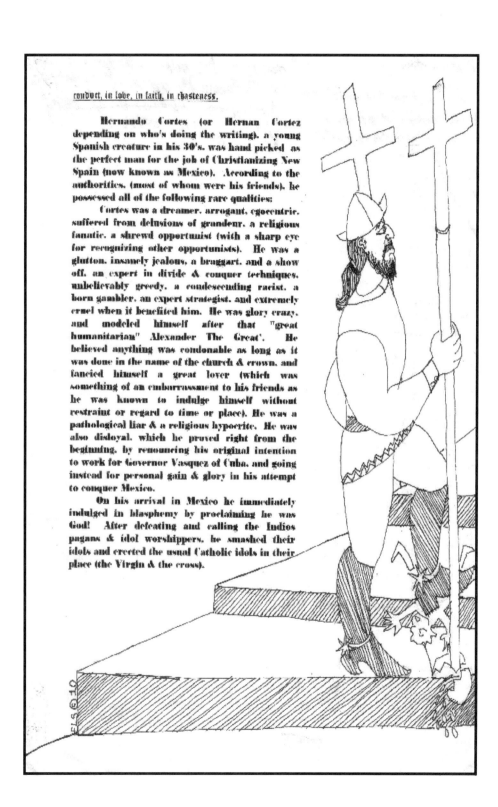

conduct, in lobe, in faith, in chasteness.

Hernando Cortes (or Hernan Cortez depending on who's doing the writing), a young Spanish creature in his 30's, was hand picked as the perfect man for the job of Christianizing New Spain (now known as Mexico). According to the authorities, (most of whom were his friends), he possessed all of the following rare qualities:

Cortes was a dreamer, arrogant, egocentric, suffered from delusions of grandeur, a religious fanatic, a shrewd opportunist (with a sharp eye for recognizing other opportunists). He was a glutton, insanely jealous, a braggart, and a show off, an expert in divide & conquer techniques, unbelievably greedy, a condescending racist, a born gambler, an expert strategist, and extremely cruel when it benefited him. He was glory crazy, and modeled himself after that "great humanitarian" Alexander The Great'. He believed anything was condonable as long as it was done in the name of the church & crown, and fancied himself a great lover (which was something of an embarrassment to his friends as he was known to indulge himself without restraint or regard to time or place). He was a pathological liar & a religious hypocrite. He was also disloyal, which he proved right from the beginning, by renouncing his original intention to work for Governor Vasquez of Cuba, and going instead for personal gain & glory in his attempt to conquer Mexico.

On his arrival in Mexico he immediately indulged in blasphemy by proclaiming he was God! After defeating and calling the Indios pagans & idol worshippers, he smashed their idols and erected the usual Catholic idols in their place (the Virgin & the cross).

21

the spiritual message of which was so strong that it was understood by all (regardless of the fact they had never heard Latin before). During this religious service these "civilized men" taught the cannibalistic savages (Los Indios,) not to eat other Indios, but that they should uplift themselves out of sin by "eating the flesh & drinking the blood of Jesus" (the holy communion.) Before the coming of Cortes only the Azteca Priests & other rare celebrities practiced ritual cannibalism, now (thanks to "civilization") everyone practiced it.

"𝕷𝖔𝖛𝖊 𝖙𝖍𝖞 𝖓𝖊𝖎𝖌𝖍𝖇𝖔𝖗 𝖆𝖘 𝖙𝖍𝖞𝖘𝖊𝖑𝖋"

Cortes on finally reaching Tenochtitlan and meeting his majesty Moctezuma, was both horrified & thoroughly disgusted. It was brought to his attention that this pagan Moctezuma actually indulged himself in the masturbatory habit of daily baths. Christianity was definitely needed here!!! No Spanish gentleman could ever practice such an obscenity!!!!!

Eventually, due to a slight mistake in judgment on the part of Cortes henchman Alvarado, the "humble Spaniards" slaughtered thousands & thousands of Aztecas while they were unarmed & involved in a religious ceremony. Needless to say, Los Aztecas could not understand that "the good Spaniards" meant no harm. Thousands, upon thousands of Aztecas popped up everywhere, and retaliated.

While the Indios were hemming in their enemies, destroying the bridges, and arranging themselves into strategic positions, the Spaniards (true to their "civilized tradition") were filling their pockets, packs, sacks & anything else they could carry with gold, silver, turquoise, pagan statues & other pagan ornaments (purely for the sake of saving heathen souls, of course.)

The Spaniards finally tried an escape, and much to their surprise found the bridges gone. They tried to swim, but rather than throw away their unholy contraband (that the Aztecas would only reclaim & use as an excuse to continue their paganism,) most of them (weighted down by treasure & crucifix) drowned. The rest, in the finest "civilized" individualistic tradition (including Cortes,) walked across the drowning bodies of their comrades.

Cortes then sat on the other side of the lake & watched the remaining few go under. They say he sat under a tree & cried (most likely saying his rosaries,) although he made no attempt to go back and help his friends. It has been debated many times by international intellectuals as to whether Cortes was crying for his lost friends, or the lost treasure. The Spaniards called this festive event "La Noche Triste" (The Sad Night,) but I'm sure the Aztecas had another name for it.

Eventually Cortes returned with the Tlaxcalans and massacred the male Aztecas. The Tlaxcalans took care of this little job of getting even with the Azteca men, while the Spaniards went about collecting gold and other trinkets, such as women (to save them from a life of sin & degradation, of course,) and we can be sure that these women were baptized immediately. It seems that Cortes made a lot of enemies by keeping the best looking women for himself (sometimes even taking those women that had already been claimed by his men), thus protecting them from falling into the hands of brutes. Any Spanish gentleman would do the same.

"Thou shalt not kill"

Cortes, having finally civilized Tenochtitlan, had time to spend on his Families. This kept him very busy, as he had a Spanish wife in Cuba, another in Mexico, and of course La Malinche as a mistress (even though he had married her off to his friend Juan Jaramillo.)

"Thou shalt not commit adultery"

Although Cortes could work very hard at mass murder, as well as slavery & adultery, he found it beneath he dignity to get his hands dirty. So he spent a lot of time convincing the Indios of New Spain that they should be Christianized, and that they should work sixteen & seventeen hours a day (whether they wanted to or not.)

He did this convincing through very "humane" and sophisticated methods, such as burning & amputating parts of bodies publicly. As a result of this type of "gentle persuasion" some millions of Indios discovered a passionate desire to convert to this civilized way of life, and voluntarily enslaved themselves. Which proves that all you have to do is reason with people, and people will work. The Spaniards type of reasoning was so successful that, even now four hundred years later some are still converting,
     and working,
        and working,
          and working,
             and working..........

"Servants be submissive to your masters with all respect, not only to the kind and gentle but also to the overbearing.

for one is approved if, mindful
of god, he endures pain while
suffering unjustly."
PETER 2:18 & 19

A VERY SUBJECTIVE VIEW OF
"OPERATION WETBACK"

It was going to be hot! Hotter than yesterday. Everyday hotter than the day before. You could see it coming .... glowing red on the eastern horizon. Freezing & shivering as we climbed on the raggedy trucks. We feared the cold almost as much as we feared the ass burning heat that was waiting for us in the fields.

Had a few quick flashes of Papi & my Tia Milagros cutting cane in Puerto Rico .... my Mother sewing stars on American flags in Brooklyn .... the Armies of no-name Ricans slaving away in the garment district in Manhattan .... Black sharecroppers all over the Deep South .... somehow this all looked familiar.

It looked like half of East L.A. & all of Mexico was climbing into those trucks. A few Blacks (including Mississippi Mo or "Sippi" .. who was married to the one we affectionately called "Wetback Lupe" we all had corny nicknames in those days.) There was a handful of Filipinos, 2 or 3 unwashed Beatniks (looking for a real ethnic experience), and me (Borinqueña negra/Employment Office reject). Folks called me "La Merengona."

Feeling scared .. lonely .. straight out of New York City, on my own .. sitting on a crowded truck .. on my way to pick fruit, vegetables, anything, because no one else would hire a 16 year old girl .. Race Black. I was a new comer to the Barrio .. an outsider .. so everybody still pretended I didn't exist. Mexican kind of Spanish sounding kind of funny/weird .. a different kind of rhythm .. strange .. not realizing that my New York Rican Spanglish sounded just as weird & funny to them. I kept looking at a lonely looking Indian dude, who kept looking at me. Looking at each other across the crowded truck. Dark .. darker than me .. his not quite American ways .. his clothes. Found out he was from Chiapas, Mexico. The local Chicanos called him "the hick", "the Wetback", "el Mayate". (With well indoctrinated Mestizo arrogance), they thought he was a funny looking "square" .. I thought he was handsome. His name was Adalberto. Look out Fresno .. ¡Ya viene East Los!

Big/loud/crude/greasy/red faced Patron grinning at us. Screaming orders in English (which most didn't understand,) telling us to work hard & we'd be rewarded. Diciendo .. "Bring all y'alls friends tamorra, we ain't got nuttin' aginst you Wetbacks! We even protects our workers here. Yassiree, all our Messy-can friends can feel right at home here!!"

As we were walking into the fields the Gringo Patron, walked up to me & Lupe, put his hairy/smelly arms around our shoulders & told us if we acted right we could even make a bonus .. "HA HA URUMRFF!" Lupe shrugged him off & walked over to her husband. I thought I heard the bastard whisper "Nigger lover" under his breath, as I spit in the dirt and ran as fast as I could into a group of teenage Chicanos, who smiled their approval at me!

In the fields I was clumsy and slow .. the joke of East Los. For each basket I filled, some 10-year-old Chicano kid filled five. I was humiliated, hot, thirsty, pissed off .. for a minute or two, I even wished I had stayed in Harlem. There, at least, I could go back to work at the Fish Market .. or maybe run some "Numbers" .. I could even steal enough to feed myself without being laughed at .. or could I .. really??

By Noon I thought I was dying. Fingers, legs, shoulders, back yelling for a rest. And my head .. aiiiii Dios, my head .. felt like the damn thing was going to split open .. Bar B Q'ed Nigger! Soaking wet .. soaking wet from head to foot. My straightened hair long gone kinky from the sweat. My first "Natural Afro" hairstyle .. sweat running out of my hair into my eyes .. blurring my vision. Frustration finally got me & I sat down & cried & cried & cried.......

Very gently .. so gently I don't know how long it was there before I felt the hand on my shoulder. Paranoid .. thinking it was the Patrón again, I balled up my fist & swung around as hard as I could .. hitting nothing but the wind. It was Adalberto, my new Indian friend. His calm black eyes smiling & without saying anything he tied a red handkerchief around my head right over my eyebrows & put his hat on my head. He took my hand, pulled me to my feet, dragged me down the row, showed me what I was doing wrong, how to do it right & silently walked away.

At the end of the day, I walked like a cripple back to the truck .. tired as hell .. but feeling super slick because there had been a mistake & I'd received credit for more than I had picked. I felt like the original Bandida Borinqueña until I looked at Adalberto. His smile let me know that those extra baskets were no mistake .. I smiled back my gratitude & handed him back his hat.

***

Mariachi music, Rhythm & Blues, teenage Chucos y sus Rucas just hanging out. Drunks & philosophers, holier than thou Church Ladies gossiping on the corners, next to Lady watching Vatos Locos .. East Los! Home again .. for a little while, at least. Mo & Lupe got straight off the truck, kissed their army of waiting kids hello & good-bye, and went straight to their other job (Swing Shift at the Soap Factory.) Adalberto disappeared. Jorge went straight to the local Cantina & got drunk!!! I had no place to go, so I walked the streets until my burning feet could take no more.

I tried to get to my little room over Señora Cruz's liquor store, without running into Señora Cruz (my Landlady.) Something almost impossible as she had the eyes of an eagle, the ears of a ciega & for some strange reason she liked me (strange, because she didn't like anyone.) I received her usual sermon about the salvation waiting for me at the local Catholic Church & how good it made her feel to know I didn't drink. I finally fell asleep looking out the window of my room at the California version of what I had run away from in New York.

Up at 3:30AM, getting it together for another day in the fields. Every muscle stiff. I must have looked like the Grandmother of somebody's Great-Grandmother .. crawling down the street like I needed a cane. Feeling like I'd been beat with a baseball bat & looking about the same. The only difference between this day & the day before was that I was wearing a hat & had a handkerchief tied around my head. No more super head aches for me!

Same shivering with the cold, but knowing it was only a matter of time before God turned on the heat & baked our brains again. Pretty much the same faces, with the exceptions of our aromatic "friends," the Beatniks.. who had long since decided that all this ethnic shit was beneath their dignity (much easier to write home to Daddy.) Same trucks .. same Adalberto, quiet, smiling at me. Same Patron, seeing only my ass & informing me that when I got tired of the fields & "Wetbacks" I could look him up (hijo de ratones .. I silently wished he would lay his Mama on some railroad tracks while he waited.) Everything & everyday the same. The same as they had always been for some & would always be for a lot more. Same fields, same sun, same work, same people. I felt angry, not knowing why. Still too young & stupid to understand the "why's" of what was happening.

The sun danced its way across the heavens, our heads, our backs. Halfway thru the day most of my stiffness was gone. I found myself more numb than stiff & more sore than tired .. my body worked like an automatic machine & I blanked out my mind, the anger. Every once in a while I'd be snatched into reality, by a word, a grito, laughter, or the many curses directed at the Patron/his Mama/ his children & his ancestors. And every once in a while Adalberto would come over, show me where I was messing up & help me get it back together. Sometimes Lupe, Mo & Jorge would come by and pat me on the shoulder, pass me a sandwich, or just let me know they cared. It was at times like that, that the loneliness would fade. But the numbness took over most of the time & I just went blank.

It was Payday & everyone was excited. As we were finishing up Adalberto came by & borrowed my High School sweater. We all then lined up in front of "Mister all-American/ apple pie/Christian/super redneck/Smith Jr." to collect our money, but it was not going to be all that easy. We stood there looking at the Patrón, who sat on the back of a truck grinning at us. All of a sudden, two carloads of La Migra drove up, jammed on their brakes & jumped out! They were followed by a van.

The shit was on .. my mind was blown .. folks were running .. women & men were crying .. everybody was screaming & I was scared! People were grabbed .. snatched .. dragged .. punched .. kicked by La Migra .. thrown into the van & driven away .. most never to be seen again. I didn't understand what was happening, but Adalberto was standing between me & Mo in my High School sweater, "giving five," saying "man, what's happening?" every five seconds until it was all over. When La Migra split, Lupe (who had become invisible) reappeared. Then those of us left got paid or got gypped. The Patrón was sitting there grinning from ear to ear, as we got on the trucks & headed back to East Los in silence. My first (but a long way from my last) experience with the sickness called "Operation Wetback".

Back in East L.A., Adalberto, Jorge & I went to eat at Lupe & Mo's house. While Lupe & I threw together a Mexarican dinner, she ran down what had happened, why it happened on Payday, Bracero Laws, Anglo lawlessness, the open slavery of Mexican farm workers, and a good chunk of my innocence died right there on Lupe's kitchen floor. Everybody said my sweater saved Adalberto's neck, but looking back I really think that La Migra just ran out of room in their jail on wheels.

***

Monday .... it starts all over again. The same corner, the same trucks, but lots of new faces .. hungry, resigned faces .. proud faces. Kept looking around for familiar smiles .. at least half of them had disappeared. I guess La Migra made quite a few house calls over the weekend. My anger so strong it hurt, but working in the fields soon brought back the numbness .. my mind went blank again .. for a little while.

One day we heard a dude died in "the Camps" .. a friend of Adalberto's from Chiapas. So we went over to check things out. ¡Aiiiii Dios! .. "The Camps!" .. The rat-trap little shacks called living quarters .. breeding farms for mosquitoes & flies (and they were everywhere) .. the things called beds, where people were supposed to sleep, there are no words to describe .. one cold water shower & water source for the whole place .. one out-house (bien perfumada), that made itself known long before you were in the Camp. Adalberto's friend's shack had torn up plastic where windows should have been. We opened the door .. it was hanging there by no more than a prayer .. there was no electricity, but there was enough light to see .. an old man laying on the floor .. an old man dead ..

looked like he was asleep .. like he had just got tired .. way too old to have to work in the fields .. should have been home in Chiapas playing with his great grand children .. looked like he just got tired & rather than lie down on the nasty thing "they" called a bed, he lay on the floor to take a nap .. an old, tired Mexican Indian man dead on the floor .. how long .. how long .. a wide awake nightmare .. a horror movie in living color .. I cried all the way back to East Los .. back to my room over Señora Cruz's liquor store .. my room, my Penthouse, down the hall from hot & cold running water & a real toilet .. my little room with the real windows, the funny curtains .. all of a sudden my little room with it's electric lamp & electric heater wasn't so little anymore.

***

We (Lupe & me) .. we got a stingy brim hat for Adalberto .. convinced him to get a "quo vadis" (a super close hair cut, popular with Blacks in the "fifties") so he'd look like a Black dude .. keep the authorities off his back .. he could have passed for my brother .. We even got him a California drivers license (even though he couldn't drive) under a real outstanding name (something deep, like Jimmy Lee Williams) .. coached him at a few slangs & answers to questions like "Can I see your Papers?" & "Are you a citizen of the U.S.A.?" It was all pretty naive, sincere but naive, since he could speak no other English & always had to go back to the fields to work (the fields being the main headquarters of La Migra.) But still we used the same type of thing to get his brother & two cousins (Noro, Rafael & Herminio) into the country .. some real small hair curlers .. a bottle of wave set .. a few borrowed "ivy league" suits .. we crossed the Border .. R & B on the radio loud .. laughing, bouncing .. we came stereotyping it all the way .. just another bunch of College "Nigras" on a holiday .. "they" didn't even look in the car.

***

Back to the fields .. still couldn't find work in the city .. but not so lonely anymore .. not so bored .. L.A. was a New World for most of us & most of our free time was spent just checking it out, having a good time, meeting new friends. Half our nights we spent looking for Jorge .. and we usually found him .. drunk .. half conscious, or unconscious .. but he was usually the first one at the trucks every morning .. every morning .. always ready to work .. every night we'd drag him home (the room next to mine) .. & he'd dream about his wife & kids in Mazatlan .. He used to tell us about them, brag about them .. he even cried about them sometimes .. people used to laugh at him, drunk, crying, a full grown man like that .. he wanted to send for them .. bring them to "The Land Of Plenty"

29

.. but somehow he just never made enough money .. couldn't speak English equaled the fields & the fields then & now equal   no money.. he never made enough money, so he got drunk & laughed the whole thing off .. everybody liked Jorge .. he was a natural clown .. a real funny man .. at least that's what they said.

***

I started tutoring some neighborhood kids in English .. Black & Mexican kids. It was an evening volunteer program in a community center. I didn't really know what I was doing & I probably learned more than I taught (I had been a pretty lousy student myself.) But still, I did a fair job & the kids dug me, so I was hired at a good salary.

I was a lucky girl .. luckier than a lot of my friends who were still in the fields everyday .. every damn day in the fields .. and even though we still saw each other every night, hung out together, danced, played, cried & laughed together .. I spent most of my time missing them .. I was crazy with missing them even when they were with me .. I tried to lie to myself .. I tried to pretend that I didn't know why I missed them .. it was like a desperate, helpless thing .. a feeling .. a pain inside me .. knowing the party was over .. knowing it was time to grow up .. knowing "IT" would happen .. never knowing when .. expecting "IT" .. waiting for "IT" .. always knowing "IT" would happen sooner or later .. and "IT" did .. more sooner than later!

***

A bunch of teen-agers from the Center came & told me to hurry .. La Migra just busted a truckload of Farmworkers around the corner .. a truckload that included Adalberto, Rafael, Herminio, Noro & Lupe .. the City Cops had to get in on it too & arrest Sippi because he punched an Immigration Cop in the mouth for slapping his wife Lupe on the behind.

By the time I got there "IT" was all over .. they were long gone .. I could feel a new kind of angry feeling & frustration growing in me .. so much stuff flying around in my sixteen year old head, so fast, so hard, so unfair .. I walked & walked & walked & walked .. trying to slow down my brain .. looking for that numbness that I used to find in the fields .. then reality hit me .. no more time for me to be a kid .. aiiiiii Dios, Lupe's kids .. I'd better go see about Lupe's kids!

Señora Cruz stopped me in front of her store & told me how, "...a bunch of dirty Wetbacks were arrested a couple of hours ago .. almost a whole truckload of "THEM" .. serves the ignorant fools

right .. drinking & fighting all the time .. all they do is make things rough on hard working, educated Spanish people like US .. wish "THEY" would stay down there where THEY belong & stop dirtying the image of those of US who've made it!!!" And through my tears, I looked deep into the emptiness of her face & asked myself ....
            ...MADE WHAT?????????????

    I walked away from Señora Cruz with East Los looking & sounding just a little bit more like Harlem.

ANANSI THE MIRACULOUS

A sometimes comical, almost always irreverent magnificent deified Spider. An invincible unapologetic sassy Trickster & legendary Folk hero originally from the Akan-Ashanti people of Ghana. Where, before he transformed & became known as "The Spider Man". He was an uncanny agile unbelievably powerful human-being, whose Mama probably simply referred to as Kwaku Anansi.

Anansi was always a clever little rascal famous for outsmarting bigger, bolder, richer, stronger & louder adversaries. And took great pleasure in making fools out of anyone foolish enough to get in his way.

During slavery in the Americas the prowess of Anansi was like a beautiful bright independent light at the end of a very long & ugly tunnel. Anansi took on mythic status among the enslaved Africans who clearly identified with the shrewdness of his trickery & cheered on his every victory. This small Spider was a serious force to be reckoned with & became a miniature super hero for the "have nots" & the down trodden & is the focus of hundreds of thousands of Folktales in more than fifteen languages.

When Anansi arrived in the English-speaking Caribbean he became female & was known as Anansi, Tanti Anansi, Auntie Anansi, Anancyi or simply Miss Nancy & being more than a little magical would sometimes transform back into a he & was called Brer Anansi. In Haiti they were known as Anansi, Areyé &/or Arenyén depending on the section of the island & can be either male or female. In the Spanish-speaking Caribbean they are always female & known by many names including Doñita Nancy & Queridita Titi Anansi among others.

The predictably unpredictable exploits of our "eight legged wonder" still rolls off tongues of tellers of tall tales everywhere from the Garifuna of Honduras, Guatemala & Belize who call him Hanasi, to the Storytellers of Brazil, Guyana, Venezuela & Panama. In St. Vincent & Tobago he's called Compé Anansi & Anansi-tori in Suriname. His praises are sung & immortalized in the literature of the Papiamentu speaking people of the Islands of Aruba, Bonaire & Curaçao where he's known as Nanzi & his wife as Shi Maria.

Anansi is immortal & is just one more example of African ingenuity & like the Negro Spirituals is a wonderful display of the clever use of double & triple entendres that helped us get our message across & make it through.

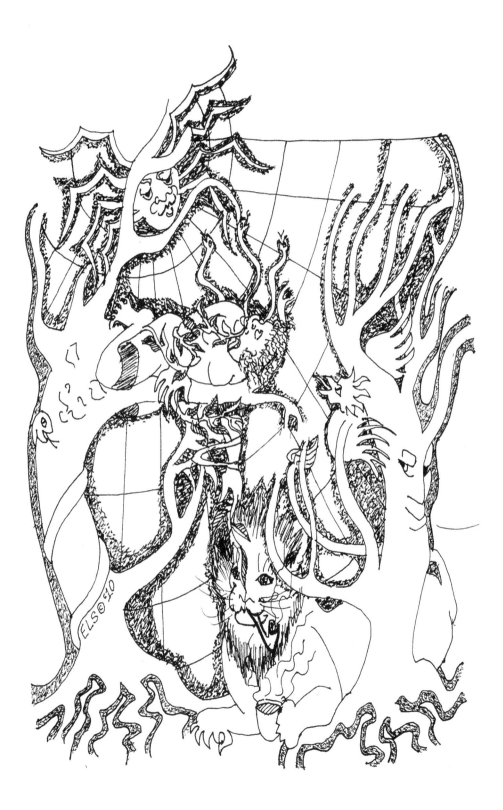

MAMA TRIED TO WARN YOU

Sleep comes sneaking around &
Creeps up on you like Anansi*
And before you know what's hit you
Slick like that cunning little Spider-Lady
Made your smart behind part of her design &
Got you trapped, caught sleeping like a baby in her web
Then turns on the powerful power of her Magic &
Takes all the locks off the pathways
To the secret worlds inside of Dreams
Sleep releases an otherworldly feast
An unpredictable uninvited supernatural banquet
A spiritual meal that balances the unbalanced
Wakes up the fantastic
Unleashes the unimaginable
And you find yourself ... wide-awake, but lost
In the inescapable maze of your own imagination
Held hostage ... Dreaming
Watching forests of singing snakes & dancing trees
Threatening hungry Lions that tease
Signifying Cheetahs & Monkeys & Gorillas
And arrogant magical Healers
A world where naughty Children forget to think
And make the same old worn out mistake
Of sinking into the trap that believes fear is a joke
Until the unreal becomes their reality &
Your dreamy fantasy becomes your Mama's worst nightmare
Full of forbidden rituals
Secret Rites ... a sacrifice you're not supposed to witness
That is, unless you're one of those chosen few who's been invited
Just another daredevil who's inviting the curse of
The Sun refusing to shine & leaving you spiritually blind
And even though that wise old Spider-Lady has
A lesson or two she's been trying to teach you
Some still don't want to listen until they're all tangled up
Somewhere trapped, scared & lost deep inside a web of dreams
Screaming & longing
For the long ignored warm arms of their Mama
Child looked so pitiful even Anansi stopped spinning
Old Girl stopped everything & put her web aside for a minute
Reluctantly laid down her latest obsessive creation
And fell down to the ground & cried & cried ... Lord she cried
Cried for all the rude & curious children

34

Children who got every thing they thought they wanted
Only to get trapped in another one of the world's beautiful webs
Locked in a deceitful nightmare of their own making
And wishing for one more chance to listen
Swearing all that is on their life to finally pay attention
And admit this time its time to wake up & do right

COMPAI PIRI, TEJEDOR DE ENSUEÑOS
(PA' PIRI THOMAS)

One day he was here
Bochinchando, pata caliente, un guapo labioso
Thought he was el rey de la calle
A wannabe tough guy
'Til he disappeared por su propia picardía
Got trapped, stopped in his own tracks!
¡Encarcelao!
Lo dejó sin conocimiento, woke up lost in a nightmare lisiado
En el cementerio endiablado de Condenadolandia
And hope took a walk, slipped quietly into hiding
Faded into an unwanted all expenses paid vacation
Gave him seven long years to think
¡Acallado!
While our side of Harlem went to sleep
¡Coño! Something was gone
For him, for us, se acabó la juventud
Then everything changed
Piri came home
He came home & turned on all the lights in Harlem
Something was different, the "wise guy" had died
And a brand new someone came home alive, on fire
Humilde, pero bien picoso
Piri was like a man pregnant with words
A walking explosion of words, Poetry on legs
Our literary Curandero singing poetic songs in Spanglish
Word/Songs, dreams
Canciones poéticas de un gran amor profundo y agridulce
Of a once inconceivable peaceful integrity
Shamelessly passionate love Songs about everyday life in Harlem
He came home with
Palabras poéticas bailando en el alma
Piri spoke & we lived for every word
Palabras y palabras y más palabras de nuevo
Líricamente cantando un canto diferente en las venas
His words turned on the lights in the eyes of Harlem
Made us see ourselves in him
See the beauty of us through him
He came back to the world a force reborn
El rey de la palabra ..... Piri,
My brother in creativity, licenciado en las calles duras
Por su ejemplo the universe sings a sweeter song

Compai Piri ..… su vida
Un gran sancocho prieto de palabras sabrosas
Especiadas de sabiduría natural
Mmm mmm mm mm mm ….. Brothaman,
What a wonderful gift for an intellectually hungry world
¡Punto!

SARSAPARILLA SCHEMING

Sistah was just an Arkansas angel
   Ebony,
      Tall,
         Fine,
And Lord knows she knew it
Just stood there, confident as the morning sun
& read me like a book
Didn't need a line,
Woman reeled me in with the music of her mind
And made me a willing pawn in her game

The Girl was Country
   Country
     & fine
       & slick
Slow & smooth & I was hooked on her music
That deep, slow Southern sound of her voice
Blues pouring out of every pore of her body
The Sistah wore desire everywhere, and
I got lost in a melodic maze of belly rubbing dreams
Schemes of how I could get closer & closer &closer

And eyes? ... Lord she knew how to work those eyes
   Sistah had those kind of
      makes you wanna jump up
       & shout kinda eyes
Irresistible eyes that made me feel all weak inside
Dark riveting eyes that hypnotized & paralyzed
Bedroom eyes that sang sweet sassafras lies
& made me want to stay awhile
Girl stared me down with passion so strong
Was nothing left to do but go wherever she was going

Felt the Poet in me
   drowning
      in the sarsaparilla sweetness
        of her Southern drawl
I forgot how to talk
Lost my voice in the easy rhythm of her arms
Charmed by the romance of her dance
I was sprung!!!
And all I could say was.....
Baby! ... Oooooowee Baby!! ... Yes Baby!!!

Lawd Baby, Baby, Baby, Baby, Baby
All night long

Yeah the girl was Country
    Country
        & fine
            & slick
And I got played, there was no way she was gonna stay
I was just another night, just another stop on the road
Just another willing pawn in her game
And just like the elusive days of Disco,
She disappeared as fast as she came

She was just an Arkansas angel
    Fallen???
        Maybe.....
            But.......
She put a smile on my face that time won't erase &
She took me all the way to heaven that night

THE RHYTHM IN US
(DRUM CALL FOR DIAMANO COURA)

In the beginning there was only the voice of rhythm
The metrical vibrations of the wind caressing a Coco Palm
A slow never ending predictable pulse
Ear candy … the reliable heartbeat of the Cosmos
It was God's dance
The medicine in every Mother's lullaby
The healing … the rhythm
The deliberate inexplicable beauty of nature's hand
A mysterious unnamable something
The hidden, but ever present, cadence of a desert storm
Forever singing to us
It has always been the rhythm keeping us alive
From the beat of our hearts to the call of the Drum
The Djembe & Djundjun dictated the sway of our Sistas hips
And the sensual swagger of our youngsters' walk
Our Children strutted their stuff like Peacocks
Flashing rhythmic wings of Gonkogui & RaRa arrogance
We were wealthy with the joy of creativity
And had no need for superficial supplements
It was all about the rhythm
The unifying power of the sound that flowed through us
Our organic Music had guts enough to be fun
Was nutritional, therapeutic & shamelessly proud

In the beginning, before the concrete clogged our ears
Before the foul scent of plastic suffocated the perfume of flowers
Even the insects in the trees sang to us
And all the rhythms of the Universe called us by name
Way back before hungry city lights gobbled up the stars
We moved with the grace of Masters on the Balafon
Kept time in a hundred different languages
And had our egos put in check by
The Berimbau, Bata Drummers & the Agogo
It was the rhythm that looked after us
Even when the going got rough & they took away the Drum
Our Fathers went into labor & gave birth to Steel Drums
Put us to bed fortified by the spiritual intensity of Mbira
Wrapped us in the storytelling prowess of the Kora & Ngoma
Told us with the Sabar to dream with our eyes wide open
And never forget it was the rhythm, it's always the rhythm
It's always going to be the rhythm

Our heartbeat … the master key … the symmetrical healing tonic
A mystical rhythmic power that clears a healthy path to total unity
Sings non-stop to the core of our Soul
This Drum Call taking us home & we are reborn in Dance!

MORE THAN JUST ANOTHER OLD TREE

When I was just a little girl, bathing in the moonstruck romantic banter of the neighborhood wild child. Old folks snidely chuckled & clucked their "holier than thou" tongues. Made all kinds of painful jokes about us. Some just thought we were being silly. Most thought we were a wee taste misled ... way too fast ... crazy but cute. "Too young to know anything about what we were talking about," they said, "How could anybody so young know anything about something as confusing & complicated as love?" "Blah blah blah blah blah!" Standing up in front of us running off at the lips, talking about us right in our faces like we weren't even there. And Lord knows those old Folks loved to hear the sound of their own voices. So they talked non-stop & talked & talked & talked. They even had the nerve to think they were so deep we couldn't possibly understand. "Blah blah blah blah blah!" But don't you believe for a second we didn't hear every single word of it. Truth was we just didn't care. We laughed & kept on playing & we kept on waiting & knew to the bone that we were meant to be together.

I promised always to you & swore forever to you. Said, "We got to hold on, I'm gonna grow into something bigger than life." I said, this is our thing & it's no Childhood fling. I knew that what was happening with us was Cosmic, something a whole lot more than supernatural. And if I could I would send my little lovesick roots deep down into the ground. I'd plant myself right outside your Mama's door ... just to be close to you. And before anyone knew what was happening, I'd come up strong. I was going to be unavoidable, something special, gigantic ... like a big old beautiful tree. And all those bad news bearing big-mouth phonies? Guess they were going to have to think again & finally take me seriously.

Several generations have passed & those two little Kids are ancient history. Just one more silly family myth about two immature "misled" lovesick kids, who never even got a chance to share a kiss. But I'm still here!!! Standing tall & proud ... standing strong! And my Soul's still grinning every time I think about your face. I can feel the magnificent power of your presence in the rhythm of your gracefulness & I'm still dancing with you any & every time the wind decides to blow. Seasons may come & seasons may go, but I'm still here singing the same old corny love song. And it's all about you.

Parents, Friends, Community ... in all their narrow-minded stupidity stood together cold like a brick wall between us. Tried to stand in our way & tried their best to rearrange our fate when we were too young to have a say. Couldn't do anything about it, all we could do was wait. But here we are, still going strong, still holding on & still unafraid. And with the birth of every brand new day, I can feel your warm kiss, your reassuring lips all over me. You are my Sun! Come to me … be with me … dependable as the morning dew. Shine down on me calm, shy & cool, but flirtatious with an insatiable hunger like a Full Moon. Come to me warm & gentle, serene as a Sun Shower. Come as an out of control Rainstorm. Caress me & passionately heal me. Rejuvenate me with the sweet medicinal essence of your wetness. Come speak to me as a Cricket. I hear your voice in the secretive whispers of Spring, in arrogant, swaggering Thunderbolts & in every Summer's breeze. Come let me dream, see the world through the eyes of every Bird that has ever nested in the tangles of my branches. Transform, shape shift, any way you want to … just come! Come … be a Squirrel … wild … running to me. Be the consistently beautiful mysterious blanket of nighttime, or come in the sugary sweet song of a BumbleBee. I don't care how you get here, just come to me! This road to together has been long & twisted, but nothing could get me to trade even one minute of it. I'd rather spend a million eternities as an old Tree in your Daddy's backyard, than have to relive the nightmare of living my life without you.

And then, when your Great Grandchild needs more than some old tired security blanket in this still insecure world let her find peace & comfort & acceptance in the shadow of an old family myth. Me … this tree … the saga of us. I hope she can feel the history of our love in me. God knows, I hope she knows I'm not just another old Tree. Let her know she's always free to run to me … like I always ran to you. And on those days when she wonders why I always feel like her very best friend … a very old, old friend. My one & only regret is & will always be that I'll never get a chance to give her the whole truth.

Hey!!!!! Maybe if you tell her. Maybe you can tell her our truth … make it your truth. Just tell her the whole-undiluted truth. I wonder if she'd even listen, much less believe it if you tried to tell her.

Hmmmmm…? Just another old Tree??? If she only knew!

STREET CHILDREN OF THE NIGHT
(PÁ LOS CHIQUITITOS DE LA NOCHE EN QUALQUIER LUGAR)

Black & brown Children of the night
Que ya no saben ná de jugar
Mis Niñitos de la calle, queridos Morenitos
Whose ideas of having fun got swallowed by the darkness
If I could
I would wrap you in sunshine
I would hold you close, enfold you in these arms
And caress whatever's left of the Child in you with lullabies
I would like to
Cover every injured inch of you
With home-cooked self esteem
En vez de deseos vacantes
I want to fill the hole that hurt dug
Take my hand, and
I'd swim defiantly through the fires of hell for you
And with you through the mugre of disrespect
I'm a hard-headed kind of Lady
And I just can't see myself giving up on you
¡Somos lo que somos! … You & I
Y para nosotros, somos todo lo que hay
We've been fused together by history
Por lo bonito y los sueños robados
Locked spiritually in the maze of our destiny
¡Oye! Mis negritos, mis pequeños callejeros
¡Los necesito!
The truth is I know I need you
Y yo sin ti, soy nada
And if I had a chance
I'd refuse to turn you loose
'Til you were so in love with yourself
That self-destruction would disintegrate
Under the pressure of your presence
And you were so secure in my love for you
And so sure of the splendor you had become
That even the Sun would lay aside its arrogance
Just to get a chance
To reflect the brilliance of your essence
And bask in the bold truth of your integrity
En ti, vive una verdad real
Y yo sin ti, no existe ni un sendero de la esperanza
Oh say can they see
You,

My beautiful wild Lotus Flowers
If I could
    I'd bathe you in a Sea of Rosewater
    I'd convert your waves of pain
    Into an Ocean of pride & faith
    Y yo te pido, dame un chance, please let me in
I promise to do the very best I can
    Even if I have to wake the dead
    And conjure up our Ancestors' breath
    I'm not too proud to act a fool, get down on my knees & holler
    And scream & beg all the Spirits of goodness to intervene
    To blow away the Fog of dismay & distrust
Pá santificar tus lágrimas & dissipate the rage burning behind your eyes
    So together we could wash away
    The centuries of emasculating doubt & de-feminizing lies
    Then have a little fun & learn to play a brand new game
    Called demolishing walls of self-hate
Children of the night
    Mis Niñitos de la calle
    I want the stubbornness of my love
    To help you turn on all the lights inside your Soul
    Tu y tu y tu ... tu eres mi sangre
I will not allow the streets of any City to steal you
    You, like a Lotus blossoming in the night
    Mis Queriditas, Alma de mi existencia
I will not allow the streets of any City to steal you
    You, like a Lotus blossoming in the night
    Mis Queriditas, Alma de mi existencia
    I will not let the cesspool of fulinga
    Make a Fast Food Happy Meal of your dreams
Chiquitos de la esquina
    You are our only wealth
    You are the most beautiful part of me
    And I'm not about to let you go
I will not permit
    The hungry stupidity of greed
    To feed you to the streets
    Without putting up a fight
    Amorcitos perdidos de la noche
If I could
    I would pave your path with Stardust
    And massage your mind with a steady diet
    Of just how important you are, make sure you know you're
    Too damn important to let the world just throw you away
It's my job to remind you on a daily basis

This crazy Old Lady is here to stay
I'm still here, staying & praying you let me in
Mis Cielitos, Negrititos de la noche
I'm talking to you ... can you even hear me???
It's our tomorrows that you're throwing away
Queridos Niñitos de la calle
I'm still waiting
A stubborn Old Lady with a heart full of love
Standing in the shadows & waiting on who you could be
Waiting for you to finally see me waiting
To wrap you in a blanket of Sunshine

THE UNRIGHTEOUS RITES
OF
REVEREND WRIGHT

Grew up on the right side of the wrong side of town. Our crazy Family was a wee taste above bottom. Our only claim to fame was the fact that we lived next door to "Reverend do right" (also known as "His Eminence" the Right Reverend Ignatius Wright). The Reverend was the unbelievably flamboyant founder & leader of "The Oasis Of Radiant Abundance". A so called new age Church which had to be the greatest scam in the land, or at the very least a free ticket to the longest running show in the city. And I mean we were close!!! Like closer than close! We were so close & those walls were so thin that you could hear an ant breaking wind in the Amen Corner.

You know, I don't like to gossip, but...... I got to tell you, the righteous Reverend was the most outrageously unrighteous, double-dealing, unscrupulous Preacher on God's green Earth. This guy was one of those infamous miracle-working Televangelist Con Artists (ooops! contemporary Media Preachers). His sermons were all fire & brimstone, intimidating scorching hell-raising rituals. High drama, well produced theatrical rites more worthy of the Academy Award than any Hollywood fantasia. His services were serialized diatribes designed to clean you out of anything you ever wished for & everything you ever worked for. And then make you feel guilty as hell & downright filthy because you couldn't give more.

Reverend Wright was about as wrong as wrong could be, but we needed his antics. In our bland land of concrete we needed the comedy of the tragedy that brought the twisted reality he offered into existence. Our lives could have easily been written off as a blank & boring slate, if it wasn't for all the shouting & tear-jerking excitement he provided on a daily basis. Life was a never-ending parade of desperate holier-than-thou sweet little old Ladies & lovely young discarded single Mamas. Sisters in the Spirit, seeking a peek at a copper-colored Holy Man who professed to really love them.

Yeah, the Boy was transparent & the promised healing purification of all the beautiful words that fell from his mouth came with a mighty price tag. But when he spoke, all the evils of the world disappeared & lives were changed & the Sisters stopped in their tracks & listened. To the folks on the street he was a sham & a clown. A common Pimp who peddled salvation for a fee, but to his congregation he was the next best thing to God & "the right Reverend" could do no wrong. Listen to his choir & Reverend Wright was a holy man whose only reason for living was to sell his flock all his divine inspirational secrets. And he figured that was just a small fee for delivering so much joy to the joyless. He & only he held the key guaranteed to absolve anyone & everyone of every transgression & wash away all sin so he could lead them to his own personal version of Heaven. And in our lower middle class Hood, his Church was the only highway to paradise & the Right Reverend sat on top of a secret combination. A sure thing, that could pull you all the way through the gates of redemption & save the most polluted of Souls.

The Good Lord knows it was a heart-breaking scene. We had a bird's eye view of that devastating day when the "good Pastor's" celestial mirage came crashing into reality. The bottom fell out of everything when the Police invaded. Looked like a battalion of the rowdiest Cops stormed in (as loud as they possibly could) right in the middle of what could have been a life altering Service. Shut down the whole operation, "cuffed" & drug "our shiftless hero" off to the County Jail! I'm sure you could hear the Ladies screaming & wailing for miles around as the Police Cars drove away.

I hate to admit it, but I miss the "old Buzzard." Truth is, he was the only show in town & these days it's been pretty quiet around here. Although for the last few years I've been hearing all these wild rumors. Stories of an aristocratic Spanish-speaking Messiah. Glorious stories about some brand new different kind of miracle-working Preacher. They say the blissful power in his voice is so healing you don't even have to understand the words he's speaking to receive the full message of his blessing. Everyone says he's a uniquely selfless spiritual Holy Man. A miracle man making big waves at this new phenomenal sounds-too-good-to-be-true kind of Church name of "El Sanctuario de Nuestra Señora Purisima de Abundancia Sagrada". A religeous Haven somewhere deep in the heart of Washington D.C. Boy's getting over big time, basking right in the shadow of the Capitol.

God knows I don't like to gossip & I don't want to start any rumors, but...... If you ask me, I'm gonna have to tell you it sure sounds like our not-so-good old friend Reverend Wright en Español!

OAKTOWN BLUE

They came on foot, by car, riding hope
On horseback, by train, on the plane
They came wearing faith, pockets full of dreams
Running from cotton fields & chopping cane
They came running, knowing better was waiting
Carrying their whole lives in paper bags
Carrying guitars on their backs
Sacks full of tall tales & Blue songs
Of a home they knew they'd always miss
But swore they'd never go back to
They came by ship ... discharged
Scarred ... wounds no time could heal
Released from military hospitals
On West Coast shores they'd never even seen
Battle fatigue ... confused ... feeling used
And they came in droves from the wars
Shell-shocked & tired & looking for a home
And when they didn't find it, they built it

On any night in West Oakland
You might run into Migrant workers
Straight out the cotton fields of Georgia
Strutting their stuff
And partying & bumpin' & grindin'
Alongside armies of Ditch Diggers
Tradespeople & unemployed Ph.D's
Who were never told they were unemployable
Saints & sinners from Texas & Mississippi
From Arkansas & Virginia
Maryland, the Carolinas
And even the West Indies
All dancing away their rage
A rage & sadness
Hidden behind memories of clouds of cotton
And buried beneath too many mountains
Of sugar cane & tobacco leaves
A frustrated fury gladly forgotten
And left behind
To rot in deserted plantation fields
And you could hear
The relief in the clubs
As Big Mama Thornton took her crown &
Gave Oakland everything ... everything

Woman gave us everything
Everything she wasn't allowed
To give in the South
John Lee Hooker
Brought the Boogie out the Delta … and
Bob Geddins, Ivory Joe Hunter & Charles Brown
Gave us smooth
You could go right down the street
And get yourself some of Beverly Stovall
Sonny Rhodes, Jimmie McCracklin, JJ Malone
Or the sophisticated sweetness of
Jimmie Witherspoon
Or the raw passion
In L.C. "Good Rockin" Robinson's Blues violin
Or get your insides ripped out
And put back together again
As Etta James & Sugar Pie DeSanto
Tore the roof off the house

The Blues didn't just slip into the Bay Area
It was like a cloud burst
The Blues came in waves
Powerful waves
Waves as subtle as a tidal wave … and
As painlessly as a pregnant woman in hard labor
The Blues came in oversized raggedy overalls
Sometimes sporting evening gowns
And 3-piece suits
It came furious, luxurious, jubilant
Overworked & underpaid
Running from the Klan
Holding on to everything they had
While others
Were just looking for something to hold on to
The Blues came West looking for freedom land
L.A., Sacramento & San Francisco had
That big city thing
Folks rocked in Russell City
Vallejo had it's scene
Richmond had a kind of
Smooth Chi-town sounding thing
But if you wanted
A gut-wrenching, soul-taking, down-home Blues
The kind, the church & your Mama
Both warned you about

The kind of Blues
That made your hair stand on end &
Snatched you out of chairs & made you shout
And jump & act a fool & dance
That good old
Makes-you-wanna-holler kinda Blues
You were gonna have to come to Oakland

Oakland ... the Blues Mecca of the West Coast
Scene was as wild or sophisticated as you were
Every place ... a different personality
And every night was party night
Where you could romance & grind
Or whine & cry about what you didn't have
Or brag & be loud & proud
And show off everything you did have
And talk about everything you wanted to be
At Slim Jenkins Club,
Esther's Orbit Room, Ruthie's Inn, or Eli's Mile High
Every night an exorcism
Where another demon was put to rest
Where you were free be real
Or be downright nasty
You could show your stuff
Til' you were wet with sweat
At the Rum Boogie, Cristie's Grill
The Paladium Club
And all the nameless
Hidden round-the-clock Juke Joints
And the Blues came down like rain
Fell down on everything
Fell down on Oakland ... where Blues was King

Then "they" came
Knocked down the cafes, tore up 7th Street
Closed the Clubs
Promised jobs & schools to uplift & save
"They" took the "Hood"
And left a wasteland full of restless spirits
Ghosts running loose
With plenty of reasons to sing the Blues
But when everyone else goes to sleep
You can still hear them
J.C. Burris, Dottie Ivory, Z.Z Hill
Mississippi Johnny Waters

Hear them singing
Their sound's written all over every building
It seeps up out of the ground you walk on
And it's yours
Little Johnny Taylor,
Johnny Heartsman
Percy Mayfield
Listen.......
They tried to free you ... they tried to heal you
With their Blues so strong
Even Willie Bobo was singing
"Never Go Back To Georgia"

Buddy Ace, Cool Papa Sadler
Brownie McGhee & Lowell Fulsom
They'll always be here
They refuse to disappear
Nothing can stop it
Gentrifiers can't block it
The same folks
That danced from the Blues scene
Into the Mambo sessions & back again
At the California Hotel
Now run to Dorsey's Locker, Bluesville,
Sweet Jimmie's & The 5th Amendment
The same people
And their children are bringing in the new
Queen Ida came
Two-stepping out the Bayou leading a Zydeco parade
And Sugar Pie DeSanto & John Lee Hooker
Never grow old
And still ride on the top of our totem pole
There's Lady Bianca & Jesse James
EC Scott & Al Von, Sister Monica
Bobby Webb & Gwen Avery
Little Frankie Lee & Billy Dunn
Wylie Trass, Faye Carol, Willie G
Frankye Kelly, Johnny Tolbert & Ronnie Stewart
Leading the Caravan Of All-stars into tomorrow

It's in the air we breathe
And it just keeps on coming
     & coming
         & coming
            & coming

And nothing & nobody can stop it
Other folks can keep their big heads stuck
Way up in the clouds
But when it all comes back down to earth
The prize is ours … & it's our jewel
& it's still coming down
Oaktown Blue

KUDUL KHELATE/THE UNCONCIOUS
(DEDICATED TO ZAK & NAOMI DIOUFF &
DIAMANO COURA WEST AFRICAN DANCE COMPANY)

The sea of the unconscious is a warehouse of Stories. Stories to remind us of all the things we have learned to forget. And of all those things we've tried so hard to leave behind. Stories full of wisdom & joy & sadness & silliness & cruelty & kindness. And every other kind of thing the wise are wise enough to admit they still don't know enough about.

It always takes a lot of courage to open wide one's eyes. You have to be very brave, or maybe a little bit crazy to really see inside a story. To really look inside, really deep, deep, deep. Deep inside the uncomfortable truth behind all the feel good lies.

Stories are the Ancestral Key. And the keepers of that Key are usually Musician, Poets, Dancers, Actors, Priests. They are the Djalis! The real Storytellers. They are the hereditary practitioners of creativity. And creativity is the mystery behind the secret of the Key. The mystical master Key to the toolbox on the sea of the Unconscious.

The Unconscious is the guardian of the magic of birth & rebirth. Of the truth, of the mystery of life & death. Somewhere in the sea of the Unconscious there's a Story begging to be told. Screaming through the Cosmos, an electrifying stream of sacred energy. A bright light screaming to be released as the unquenchable heat in some Dancer's feet. And right this minute it's singing to me. Demanding I ask for permission to share that vision with you. I can feel it coming through.....

A long, long, long time ago, there was in Liberia a village of women. They were the So So women. Women who sang & danced & carved the most beautiful canoes. The fishnets they wove were exquisite. So amazingly intricate, that even Anansi the arrogant spider was intimidated. And jealously crazed with rage by the incomparable beauty of their skill. These women cleared the land & built magnificent huts. Planted the best of seeds & harvested bountiful crops.

In this village of women. A long, long, long time ago, in a land called Liberia there was a Chief. A woman Chief. A regal, but lonely Chief. She was a stern task master, whose rule was absolute. An overbearing power shared only by her loyal assistant. A moody, ever-present, overworked, omnipotent Spirit. This Spirit was the eyes & the ears & the enforcer of the traditional order.

When the Chief spoke ... the Spirit listened & acted immediately on her behalf. And the one & only response accepted for her every request was yes!!! Until that fateful day she came face to face with a shrewd, sensual, playful Dancer. A handsome stranger, brave enough to say no & stubborn enough to refuse to go. He couldn't be chased away.

Now there's a whole lot more that you need to know. But the only way to come to the end of this Story is to open the doors to your mind & see with your heart & feel with your eyes. And you'll find the path with all the answers in the Rhythm & the Dance.

One Story is always winding down, while another one comes to life. The Unconscious is a treasure chest of tall Tales waiting to run wild. And swim Seas full of homesick ghosts that roam the Ocean's floor. Stories that come alive celebrating & partying & mourning in the morning dew on the leaves of every tree. Hundreds of Stories that stagger around drunk & get buried alive. Tall Tales destroyed & lost in the numbing fog of Palmwine dreams.

And in the forest of one more West African village a brand new bigger than life legend is being born. A love Story. A Story of revenge. A Story about beauty & demons. About weddings & treachery & the deepness of secrets. It might even be a Story about you.

A good Storyteller is always looking for a new Tale to tell. In the world of the Unconscious, the Stories never end & the sea of imagination never ever goes to sleep. There's a Story in the Music & in every word a Poet speaks. It's in your Church, in every Mosque. It plays with Kids in the Sandbox & it's in your Barbershop. You've even got out-of-control Homie Stories running buck wild in the streets.

The Unconscious is an unending sea. A warehouse of creativity & somewhere in that Sea, there's a whole new Story waiting its turn to be told. Like a sonic beam, it's screaming through the Cosmos. An inescapable stream of sacred energy. A bright light beaming & right now it's trying to speak. It wants to shine on you. I can hear it singing to me. To you ... to all of us. Demanding we find the time to keep the creativity of this tradition alive.

It's going to take monumental courage to walk through life with your eyes wide open. You got to be brave ... don't be afraid. Be crazy enough to climb inside a Story & let that Story get inside of you. Have the guts enough to be special enough to give a tall Tale a chance to grow, not knowing where it's going to end.

If you come with us ... you'll grow with us.
You'll find the path to all the answers in the Rhythm & the Dance. The path is always there. It's always been there ... waiting for you to come ... waiting for you to see. It's somewhere ... deep, deep, deep in the Unconscious. Dive in ... take a chance! You'll find every single answer that you seek wrapped in all the glorious Stories. Hidden in the Rhythm ... living in the Dance.

And if that's still not enough & you really want to know some more. Guess we're gonna have to see you at our next show!

COSMIC SOUL MATES
FOR
ALICIA PIERCE, ELEO POMARE, SYLVIA DEL VILLARD,
PEARL PRIMUS, GREGORY HINES & KATHERINE DUNHAM
WHOSE TRUTHS ARE CLOTHED IN DANCE

Time
Is a Dancer
Moving
Shamelessly
Through the Cosmos
The wise
Hear the call
In their bones
&
Become willing partners
Trying
Always to follow the lead
Of
The inexplicable forces
Which propel
The mystical beauty
Of its truth on its journey
Time
Is a Dancer
Moving
Proudly moving
Flowing
Eternally cognizant
That the alternative is
A guaranteed voyage
Into
The annals of obscurity
A nowhere land
Where
Even time forgets to dance

60

THE TRUE QUEEN OF CARNIVAL
A TRIBUTE
TO "CONNIE" CONSTANCE WILLIAMS
(3/14/1905-10/13/2002)

You know, even now eighteen years later, I still can't walk down Fillmore without my mouth starting to water. My brain still filled with the taste of Connie's curried goat & an unsatisfied craving for Connie's coconut bread. And sometimes I can even hear the "Pan Music" that used to fill the street when you came anywhere near Connie's West Indian Restaurant. There are times when I wonder whether it's really the food, or the music that I miss, or is it really the intellectual, political, cultural, freedom & spiritual stimulation??? But I guess I've put the cart in front of the horse. Maybe I'd better start at the beginning… Maybe I'd better say something about this Connie & who she is & why she's so firmly implanted in my being!

Constance A. Williams, AKA "Connie", was born March 14, 1905 in the city of Port Of Spain, in the island nation of Trinidad & Tobago. Her Grandparent on both sides had come from Tobago, bringing their many children, including 3 sets of twins (one of which was her Father Johnny). When Connie talks about her childhood in Trinidad, it seems as if she could go on forever about the lush beauty of the island, her love of her Grandmother & the fun & games she played with her friends. Still, underneath all her talk of Trinidad's overwhelming beauty, there's always this feeling of sadness. Much of which I'm sure comes from her missing her Father (her parents split up when she was very young, and her Father moved to New York).

Connie was a shy, but stubborn child, who it seems that fate had chosen to surround with the Arts. Her landlord "Old man Scott" was a great Storyteller, and the Great-Grandfather of the legendary Jazz pianist & Vocalist Hazel Scott, who later became the wife of Adam Clayton Powell Jr. One of her best friends Auguste, the neighborhood terror by her own admission, became an Actor as a youth. The Arts just always seemed to gather around Connie, and whether she intended it or not the Arts wouldn't let her go. So they followed her to the U.S.A.

In April 1924 Connie made "the big move" to New York so she could reunite with her Father. She didn't know that "the big move" would be far bigger than she was prepared for. It had been a very cold winter, and there was still snow on the ground. In other words it was freezing, and Connie being one of the Caribbean's tropical daughters had none of the right clothes (she didn't even have any boots). Still, just being able to see her Father made Brooklyn bearable. She began to hear about all the "Trini" doings up in Harlem, and eventually moved there to be closer to other Trinidadians.

When she got to Harlem she realized that she really didn't know how to do anything, so she began Babysitting. Then the War (World War II) broke out, and she like a lot of other women began working on the Assembly Lines in New Jersey. The women would be picked up in the morning and driven to New Jersey, and evenings she'd go to school. It was at that school that she met her first love... cooking!

She began cooking for friends, and her place became "the" hangout for hungry Artists & intellectuals. When it became apparent she was spending more than she could afford, some of her friends told her she should open a restaurant, a place where people expected to pay. The hunt began, and eventually wound up in Greenwich Village when she found an abandoned two-room basement that had once been a restaurant. Connie says, "I had a lot of nerve! I didn't even have the money for a down payment, so the Landlord gave me the first month free. There were lots of old tables & chairs & plenty of dirt. With the help of my friends, I just started cleaning and the next thing you know The Calypso opened its doors!"

In 1941, when The Calypso opened in New York, times were hard for most and many businesses fell apart, but thanks to Connie's cooking and the Artistic & Caribbean gossip lines The Calypso was an instant success. It would take more time and space than I have here to give the whole story on how the miracle of The Calypso's success came into being, but it became "the place" to be. Everybody who was anybody, rich or poor, of every color imaginable hung out at The Calypso. And when I say everybody, I mean everybody, from Park Ave. to the park bench!

One of those people was Stan Weir, a long time Socialist Trade Unionist, writer, and publisher, who said, "James Baldwin and I came to Manhattan's Greenwich Village by separate ways in the third year of World War II. He was eighteen, but knew that there was no other life for him than that of a writer. I was twenty-two, a Merchant Seaman temporarily ashore. We were introduced by Connie Williams, a Trinidadian restaurateur who was about to open her new cafe, The Calypso. She had recently told her friend and well known Artist, Beauford Delaney, that she needed a waiter and to send her anyone he thought would be good. Delaney sent Baldwin. When I returned to The Calypso in the late afternoon Connie greeted me with the announcement that I was to be a temporary dishwasher and her then waiter, Jimmy, and I were special boarders. Then she introduced us. A unique yet natural adoption process had been set in motion.

"At first Baldwin was shy, but soon we had long discussions. It was not just the talk and the good food that quickly laid the basis for our friendship. The Calypso was catching on fast in a unique segment of the public, especially among radical intellectuals. C.L.R. James, for an example, sometimes brought Pan Africanists; Beauford Delaney attracted the Henry Miller crowd; and then there were the dancers, musicians, actors and singers from the equivalent of what are now the off-Broadway shows — many were West Indians carrying developed political attitudes.

"A common bond among many of these regulars was the feeling that the heads of state in both Russia and the United States were incapable of leading the world to more personal freedom and were part of the problem. It is improbable that there were many places in that city where people were genuinely entertaining each other, and as an extension of their enjoyment, discussing politics.

"Neither Baldwin nor I had ever before been with people who shared their artistic and social talents so generously, almost as a regular ritual. We joined the discussions and after-hours parties both as equals and awed apprentices. He had grown up in nearby Harlem hampered by narrow opportunity to socialize with people of his own age. Until 1940, I had spent my entire life in East Los Angeles, a product of the big band era. The distances we had traveled to were close to equal. Just as important, this was the first time either of us had been allowed extended face to face access to a person of 'the opposite' race and the same generation."

Yes, The Calypso was a special place, a safety zone in a world that seemed to be upside down, and on any day you might run into Marlon Brando (who at that time, according to Connie, "was just a kid in blue jeans who wanted to be an Actor") or you might see the great Be-Bop innovator Charlie "Yardbird" Parker, Langston Hughes, Eugene O'Neill's two sons Sean & Gene Jr. Writer Claude McKay was a regular. You might run into Actor Dick Huey, Composer Clarence Williams, Frederick Douglas Wilkerson, and even Eleanor Roosevelt. The Calypso was right around the corner from Katherine Dunham's Studio, so many of her Dancers, students, fans, and Musicians would be there. And even I knew about The Calypso, though it took many years before I actually met, and became aware of how important Connie Williams was & would become in the history of Trinidadian influence in the U.S.A.

If you were looking for good food you went to The Calypso. If you needed to find out where you could find the latest in Caribbean music, you went to The Calypso. You might even run into the great Calypsonians Mac Beth (who was the most popular Calypsonian in New York at the time and I believe was the Father of percussionist Ralph MacDonald), or Lord Melodie (the mastermind behind the Calypso hits of Harry Belafonte) or The Duke Of Iron (of Pretty Woman, and Don't Stop The Carnival fame.)

The Calypso was always alive & at the center of it all you'd find Connie. The woman always appeared tooooooo busy working to notice anything else, but believe me Connie was conscious of and many times orchestrating the very activity she appeared too busy to notice. There was very little that happened at The Calypso that Connie was unaware of. That awareness of Connie's was one of her best & worst traits. It meant that she knew when all was well, but was just as aware when someone was troubled or hungry. And Connie, being who she was, considered it her duty to take care of & cure the problem, no matter how strange it was. If you were a friend of Connie's, then Connie was a friend of yours! So she wound up feeding many a hungry Artist, and even covering up one woman who chose to disrobe publicly on a regular basis. She even paid the rent for one of the greatest Artists this country or the Caribbean has ever known when he was sick. She eventually became aware (if she was ever really unaware) that she was probably putting out more money than she was taking in. And that she was just repeating the same script that she had played out when her apartment had been the place to hang out... only now it was bigger! But Connie Williams is Connie Williams, and she would go the grave believing that every hungry mouth should be fed. She, therefore, continued to do as she'd been doing, and to this day she's yet to regret any of it.

Fate has its own way of taking care of business, and N.Y.U. (New York University) wanted the entire block that housed The Calypso. You can't keep a good woman down, so Connie just moved... this time to California. She tried to duplicate her accomplishments in New York on the West Coast, and the first real Caribbean style Carnival & restaurant appeared in Santa Rosa, California in 1956. Needless to say, without the Caribbean fire it didn't work too well, so she came to San Francisco!

In San Francisco, like New York, there is a very strong West Indian/ Caribbean/Latin American and artistic presence, and Connie was immediately embraced by both. In 1961 Connie's West Indian Restaurant opened on Haight Street. It was at the beginning of the Flower Power Era, and the area was alive with peace, love & happiness. Connie was in her element, that is until the tourists & drugs came in and destroyed the dream.

By this time Connie had developed quite a following, so when conditions dictated she just moved the whole operation onto Fillmore Street. The restaurant opened in 1964. And if you came in anytime between 1964 and the day she retired in 1974, you might run into the greatest Artists, Radicals, or Politicians on the West Coast. Lt. Governor Mervin Dymally, Assemblyman Willie Brown (who's now Mayor of San Francisco emeritus,) Val Serrant (one of the greatest Steel Pan Drummers of all time,) Senator Milton Marks, Benny Velarde (who's played with everyone in Musica Latina including Cal Tjader,) George Leong (founder of the S.F. Asian American Jazz Festival,) Debra Vaughan & Elendar Barnes (Dancers/Choreographers & co-founders of Oakland's Dimensions Dance Theater). Poet Pat Parker, and Musician/ Educator Carlos Frederico (one of the founders of the infamous Mambo Sessions at The California Hotel,) the indescribable Mongo Santamaria. Writer & Educator Angela Davis, Blues icons Sonny Terry & Brownie McGee, Jazz great John Handy, and Dance-world legend Ruth Beckford, Rahsaan Roland Kirk, Lord Melody, Dancer Adela Chu (who later became the founder of Hawaii's Carnival,) "Bobi" Cespedes (lead singer & co-founder w/ her brother Luis of Conjunto Cespedes, as well as the Carnavalito, a children's Carnival in the Bayshore Hunter's Point district,) and myself Avotcja (of KPOO & KPFA,) as well as Patrick Prescod (one of the Caribbean music pioneers in California.) Then Mayor Moscone was a regular, Rev. Cecil Williams & S.F. Poet laureate Janice Mirikitani, and Jazz legend Mary Lou Williams. And last, but definitely not least, I must mention Gloria Toolsie (who was not only one of the most regular of regulars & a "some time" employee, but also one the most creative costume designers & Dancers outside of the Caribbean, as well as one of the finest cooks I know.) Gloria's Mother (also from Trinidad) and Connie had been long time friends, and when Connie & Gloria got together it was only a matter of time before they would change Bay Area history forever!

One day I was hanging out in the kitchen of Connie's Restaurant, and heard Connie & Gloria put together the entire plan for San Francisco's first Carnival while they were cooking & preparing food. The year before (1964), they had put on the first Calypso In The Streets & left us all wanting for more & more & more & more! So they gave us more. San Francisco's first Carnival was born in the kitchen of Connie's West Indian Restaurant, and came to life on the streets of the "Western Addition." It was truly a community affair (which is what a true Carnival should be) and it got bigger & bigger, and eventually moved up to Mission Dolores Park. It continued to get bigger over the years, and we knew we wouldn't have to wait long before it was taken out of the hands of the community that gave it birth.

Next thing we all knew, Carnival was moved Downtown, then back to the Mission District where it remains, and everybody but Connie & Gloria are given credit for it's birth. Folks have gone all around the world to find Kings & Queens for San Francisco's Carnival, and not once have the powers-that-be even acknowledged Connie Williams or Gloria Toolsie. How sad!!! Connie has awards & plaques from the San Francisco Board Of Supervisors, Lt. Governor Mervyn M. Dymally, Mayor George Moscone, The San Francisco Black Teachers Caucus, Assemblyman Willie Brown, The African American Historical & Cultural Society, etc., stating that she was the founder of Carnival. Connie has a large suitcase, full of awards naming her as the creator of Carnival in San Francisco. She's been acknowledged by everyone, but the Carnival Committee itself. Something is very wrong with this picture!

History might have been rewritten if we had all faded away and remained quiet, but fortunately that hasn't been the case. As I said earlier, fate has a strange way of working things out. I became very ill, and although I was unaware of it Connie was also very sick at the same time, and we lost touch with each other. Gloria had moved out of the State, and things Caribbean had become very quiet. But every time I'd walk down Fillmore I'd start thinking about Connie & craving her coconut bread. Sometimes I'd even stop and look at the place where Connie's West Indian Restaurant used to be, and I'd remember all those happy days when I'd either be eating or working or just hanging out in the kitchen talking with Connie & Gloria & my Children. And then one evening, who walks into one of my Gig's (I play Music & write Poetry), but Connie. I was in seventh heaven! Until I went to Carnival a few weeks later, and realized Connie wasn't even mentioned in passing in any of the Carnival literature, and they had imported a Carnival Queen (who had just played at the then boycotted Sun City, South Africa). This story could have ended on a very sad note, but miracles do happen!

I got angry & started talking about Connie everywhere! And then a Trini friend of mine, Dancer Jackie Artman, dared to act on the information. According to Jackie, "I had been hearing about Connie. My Aunt Bernadette Hercules was part of the first S.F. Carnival, along with Gloria Toolsie. Without Connie, the whole Carnival movement would not exist! It struck me as being very unfair, after putting all that into it, she wasn't even acknowledged!" So rather than wait for someone else to do something, Jackie made sure that Connie was acknowledged at every Carijama (Oakland's Carnival) since it's inception in 1984. Thanks to Jackie's efforts, Connie has received awards at the Caribee Dance Center, and has been paid tribute to at the 1991 Trinidad & Tobago Independence Day Celebration at Oakland's California Ballroom (which is especially significant, as Connie worked at pulling the first Trinidadian Independence Celebration in the Bay Area together many years ago & featured Calypso super star Lord Melodie.)

Life is strange, and even though Connie Williams has begun to receive some of the acclaim she is due, she still is an invisible entity in San Francisco's Carnival. I hear that things are changing. I hear things about a letter writing campaign, about petitions, etc. Only time will tell the full story.

As for me, Connie will always be one of my heroes. I was not raised to turn my back on those who tilled the soil upon which I walk! To quote myself, "Some of you might remember Connie Williams from Connie's West Indian Restaurant on Haight, or Fillmore in San Francisco, or maybe even The Calypso in New York. I've eaten a lot of coconut bread in my life, but none has ever touched Connie's! In her hands, food became a sacred ritual. ...Connie's wasn't just a restaurant, it was a very active community center, both social & political. It was a West Indian Community Center, the first of it's kind in the Bay Area. And the first Carnival in San Francisco was born there. Connie wasn't just a brilliant cook, her heart was as big as her culinary expertise, and if it hadn't been for her a lot of folks (including my children & I) might have starved to death! Connie cared & walked her talk. She was always very outspoken & highly political. Connie was so popular that when a racist reviewer tried to slander her in the Bay Guardian newspaper, there was uproar so loud that it could be heard in the Black, Latin, Asian, and White communities. People started bombarding me with phone calls at both of the radio stations I work at, and after checking it out my research resulted in the documentary, "¡Cuidao! Tourist Loose In The Ghetto!" The critic disappeared, but Connie's still around & after a long battle with Cancer looks as beautiful as ever. She's still a great supporter of the Arts, and I've taken her to see The Jolly Boys of Jamaica, Calypso Rose of Tobago, as well as many other places & would be honored to take her anywhere else she chooses to go!

Recently (due to my refusal to give up and much needed help from Jackie Artman & THE ALL A WE POSSE of the East Bay), Connie has finally been declared the founder of and real Queen of Carnival (even though she still hasn't received any recognition from San Francisco's Carnival Committee.) She's been getting some attention from TV & the print media, as well as the museums, and her presence has become a must at all West Indian events.

Connie no longer has her restaurant, and due to the harsh financial reality we now live in, she now lives in the Tenderloin District of San Francisco. It wouldn't be so bad, except after feeding & taking care of so many of the "who's who set," nobody's taking care of her! Only James Baldwin remembered until the day he died, as well as Poet Janice Mirikitani, and a couple of others. Everybody else is too busy making money, and it makes me sad, real sad. ....But Connie??? When I asked her how does it make her feel, she says, "I've lived my life as I wanted to & it's been a good life. Money????? They'll die, and leave the money. ..they can't take it with them! I've lived a long life & I've had many good friends like Jimmy Baldwin, Claude McKay, Lord Melody, Harry Belafonte, etc.." What a blessing to be part of that number!!!

Connie Williams, I love you!!!!! And to me, you'll always be.........

The True Queen of Carnival!!!!!!!!!!!!!!!!!!

NOTES

Quote from Stan Weir taken from an article that appeared in "Against The Currant" January/February 1989

And where I've quoted myself, taken from my article "Pan Africanismo Musical" - Reggae Calendar International, San Francisco March 1991)

LA DANZA DEL VAMPIRO

Fue el
De nuevo
Fue el
Otro renacimiento del mismo demonio hermoso
El mismo basurero vestido en esmoquin bien parecido
De nuevo
Corrupción malicioso envolvio en paquete regalo
Maloliente como siempre, pero
Elegante y bien hablado ... ¡Un tipo rabiosio!
Un malvado atractivo bailando en su lecho de muerte
Fue el
Un monstruo goloso
Vampírico, malgenioso ilimitado y sin compasión
Fue el
De nuevo
Se escapó el vampiro desesperado pá poderío sin igual
Estupidamente un tonto hambriento lo despertó
Se levantó de su dormir ... se levantó arrebatando almas
Y te invita a bailar ... Te necesita pá bailar
Su canto ... una llamada a las garras de la muerte
Su canto tan lindo ... una cancion azucarada
Otra cosita linda pá meterte en su danza
Fue el
Y llegó buscando y sediente de sangre
Mas sediente de antes y loco de poder
Odioso, indeseado y lleno de deseos sobornados
Fue el
Que comio la lengua de Victor Jara en Chile
Fue el
Disfrutando y tirando bombas
En la iglesia con las 4 chamaquillas de Alabama
Fue el
Bailando en las sombras de los muertos de Iraq y Kosovo
Estaba el mismo vampiro
Manejando por las calles de Jasper, Texas y Cambodia
Fue el
Rodando en Haiti, Nicaragua, en Ruwanda y Uganda y
Bailando por la destrucción en Grenada y Panama y
Rompiendo la paz de nuevo
De la gente indigena de Australia, Chiapas y Argentina
Fue el

Bailando en el sendero mortal del diablo con el Nazi
Y fomentando la muerte, destrucción y locura
En Palestina, Oklahoma, East Timor y la Ciudad de Nueva York
Y te invita a bailar ... Te necesita pá bailar
¡Cuidado! ¡¡¡No te duermas!!!!
Su raro desaparecimiento es nada mas que
Otro pequeño tiempo de maquinar su proximo ataque
¡Cuidao! ¡Abran los ojos!
Todavia te necesita pá bailar, pero
Se va a equivocar, si cree que voy a bailar su Son
¡Conmigo ná!
Ni su propio veneno le daria a tomar
Pá ese monstruo endemoniado ... no tengo ná
Pues quizás...
Solo un membrecia vitalicia en un Banco de Sangre
Un Banco lejano
Un Banco de Sangre irresistible y bien lejos de mi

DANCE OF THE VAMPIRE

It was him
Again
It was him
Another reincarnation of the same old handsome demon
The same old garbage can wearing a brand new tuxedo
Again
Sneaky & vicious ... gift-wrapped corruption on legs
Still smelling just as bad, but
Talking sweet & walking elegant ... Dude's insanely evil
A wicked attractive evil dancing on a bed of death
He's here again
A cold blooded, greedy monster
Unfeeling, blood thirsty, with zero understanding
It was him
Again
The vampire's loose, desperate & power tripping
The stupidity of a hungry fool woke him up
He got up snatching souls
& he's asking you to dance ... He needs you to dance
His song ... an invitation into the jaws of death
His beautiful song ... a sweet sugar covered song
Another pretty little thing to pull you into his dance
It was him
And he came searching ... thirsty for blood
Power crazy & more thirsty than ever before
Hateful, unwanted & full of twisted desires
It was him
He's the one who ate the tongue of Victor Jara in Chile
It was him
Having himself a good old time ... throwing bombs
In that church with those 4 little girls in Alabama
It was him
Dancing in the shadows of the dead of Kosovo & Iraq
It was the same vampire
Driving the streets of Jasper, Texas & Cambodia
It was him
Hanging out in Haiti, Nicaragua, in Uganda & Rwanda &
Dancing through the ruins of Grenada & Panama &
Tearing down the peace again
Of the indigenous folks in Australia, Chiapas & Argentina
It was him

Dancing down the devil's deadly path with the Nazis
Encouraging death, destruction & madness
In Palestine, Oklahoma, East Timor & New York City
You better not go to sleep!!!
His occasional disappearance is nothing more than
Another piece of time to plan his next attack
Be careful! ... Don't close your eyes!!!
He still needs you to dance, but
He'll be making a big mistake
If he thinks I'm fool enough to dance to his tune
I don't want anything to do with the Dude!
I wouldn't even give him a drink of his own poison!!
For that fiendish monster I got nothing!!!!!
Well maybe...
Just Lifetime Membership in a Blood Bank
A distant Blood Bank
An irresistible Blood bank that's a long way away from me

THE UNSEEN SIDE OF GENTRIFIED

Busy, busy busy, busy, busy!!! The City was always busy, always in motion, never slowed down. The place never stopped! And everyday the whole City, smugly comfortable in its blindness, walked by "them." Tried not to see "them" & when their eyes couldn't avoid "them," their feet just seemed to walk a little bit faster & faster & faster until they passed "them" by. "What you don't see just can't be." It was an everyday ritual. Said "they" were just another blemish on the already somewhat tarnished egocentric reputation of the Country's most infamous City. Said "they" were an eyesore. But that was just one part of one more excuse for those "good immaculate upwardly mobile Church-going folks". You know, the kind of folks who were always looking for any excuse they could use to look down on anything or anyone who wasn't doing exactly what they thought should be done the way they thought everyone should be doing it!

These Slums, these endless blocks of condemned Tenements were the worm in "The Apple." Buildings were supposed to be empty. City had condemned them years ago. Was really some kind of gentrification game! The end result of the latest edition of Big Money versus Old Money warfare. You know... get rid of the Tenants "any way you wanna" & after watching all the transparent scams for "new" ownership play out & after waiting the legally appropriate amount of time... REMODEL!!! Jack up the rent & import Suburbia. Oh yeah, same ole same ole! Translate that sick, slick "BS" into "relocation of the savages!!!" Another day another dollar!

But everybody didn't go, wouldn't go. Deal was there was nowhere they could go. Most were everyday people who had lived there for generations. All kinds of people. There were whole families, hundreds of families, living in unacknowledged invisible cities. Families that refused to accept the illogical logic that declared them disposable, unneeded, replaceable, erasable. Inside those closed up buildings was a whole universe of invisible cities within the City. Each one of those buildings, a world of the good, the bad & the ugly. A world where the Sanctified & Sinners, flamboyant Drag Queens, hard-working Family men & guys that seriously worked hard at not working, made peace with discarded Senior Citizens & angry abused runaway Kids & mad & sad throw away Kids & just plain wild & crazy thrill-seeking adventurous Kids running in place to create a home of their own. These buildings were alive & full of old road-weary Hobos, proud unbreakable single Mothers, wanna-be Pimps that got pimped, street corner Preachers & desperate Dope Fiends. These condemned buildings were alive with Black Nationalist pride, warring Clans of Gypsies & several families of Iroquois whose every breath was a declaration of Red Power.

Before he saw her, Mario was numb, was a dead man, was walking around lost in Central American dreams. Felt like he was buried in hopelessness. Homeless, hungry, homesick & whipped by loneliness. So broke & tired he almost forgot how to feel. Nobody ever talks seriously about the dignity, or any kind of old fashioned pride, or of real love affairs in old condemned buildings, but that's where it happened. Mario fell in love with an angel in the middle of what he thought was his Armageddon! At first he couldn't believe she was real ... but she was. Knew she couldn't be possible. And if she was, knew she wouldn't be interested in anybody like him, but her smile told a different story. She was smart & sassy & the classy beauty of her Blackness dazzled him. Turned the lights on so bright, they wiped out a lifetime of his Mama's "color line" lies. And the music of her children's laughter made him glad he was alive.

And then there was the Reverend Mother Eula Jean Combs, an ex-Hooker that got "hooked." Found God when she lost herself in a maze of Drugs & madness so low that no one but the Lord would stick out their hand to pull her up. The Reverend was a regal, Pentecostal, storytelling, singing type of Preacher with a very religious, overzeal-ous, proselytizing, full congregation who held Church right there in the building every night. EVERY ... SINGLE ... NIGHT!!!!!!! Much to the dismay of the "Crack Monsters" down the hall & the louder than loud Break-Dancing Hip Hoppers & renegade Graffiti Artists & teeny bopper Punk Rockers upstairs & the irony of an army of legal & illegal Asian immigrants who shared the floor below with Bernie, an "out to lunch" delusional Vet who had gone to war & lost his soul.

And every one of these groups thought they were better than the other, looked down on the other, made fun of each other, actually hated everything about each other. And that was the way it always was, until there was a fire, or a suicide, or some other major catastrophe. Like an Election year, when the Authorities had to grandstand & come down in self-righteous indignation on one of its almost predictable well-publicized raids. And all of a sudden everyone remembered they were neighbors & did what had to be done to make sure everyone got out alive with as much as was humanly possible. Then very efficiently counted heads & made sure each & every body was safe (especially the Old Folks & Children.) After which came the unbelievable job of everyone helping everyone to move back in as soon as the coast was clear. And as soon as they were settled, without blinking an eye, they all went right back to wearing that same old negative venom & animosity like it was some kind of uniform.

These buildings, in this universe of invisible cities within the City, were a safety zone for those who'd been wrongfully evicted & those who were so despicable they would have even been evicted from

Hell!!! These buildings, for better or worse, were a neutral zone for the disillusioned & suicidal & sweet little old Ladies running from the lifeless absurdity of living hidden away from life in some Old Folks' Home & flaming Drag Queens & tired, disoriented, homeless Veterans & hoards of homeless, working poor & overworked burned-out homeless Housing Rights Activists; all trying to make some kind of life for themselves. A place where folks were forced into protecting each other whether they wanted to or not. Necessity made their bed & was the only thing holding them together. Maybe that lumpy bed was the only real democracy in the whole Country.

But the City?!? The City was so busy, so comfortably blind behind the mask of its own hypocritical bourgeois sophistication... it never even noticed.

ELIXER OF NZINGA

Armies sailed oceans
Riding inside the indescribable waves of my uncontrollable tears
My tears … transplanted African tears
The spice that put the soul in Soul Food … the inescapable key
Our spiritual fuel
The diet that fired up Chief Osceola, caused the Seminole Wars
Legalized Slave Traders stealing his Wife was the real reason
Stealing his Soul-mate … his Woman … the final straw
It was my tears,
Fed hundreds of Invisible Conductors
On the ever moving Underground Railroad
From quiet Quakers to the loud fervor of John Brown to
The proud invincible determination
Of that beautiful no quitting Sister Harriet Tubman
My African tears,
Fed on "Ain't Gonna Let Nobody Turn Me Around!"
Swallowed & digested & converted all that pain
That terrible weight … that inhumane burden
That hole in the soul
The secret of our heat & our Cool when society's stone cold
Strong healing waters … Nzinga's Elixer … stronger than dread
Put a damper on the handcuffs of fear &
Cleansed & freed our hearts & fed our souls
From Surinam to Trinidad to Curacao
To ain't no stopping us now Mississippi
Fueled Jamaica's Granny Nanny
El Negro Falucho in Argentina
Colombia's Benkos Bioho de Palenque &
Haiti's Toussaint L'Ouverture
We swam through hell on that ocean of tears
At times, the sorrow so loud
Even the night screamed & the clouds cried
And the rain fell down from the sky, red with blood
These tears have irrigated millions of acres
Of Cotton, Coffee, Yuca, Breadfruit & Sugar-cane
They've seasoned your Grandma's Greens
Titi's finger licking Lechon & Uncle Lalo's Curried Shrimp
They are in the sweet taste of Flan & Callaloo &
Every piece of Coconut Bread & all the Wheat that you eat
These tears have followed you
From the Favelas in Brazil to Haiti's Lavalas
Fertilized the anger hidden behind the tired smiles
In every after hour Juke Joint & Cantinas del Solar &

Bob Marley's mysticism
In Estevanico's so called discoveries &
Beethoven's remarkable Symphonies
La Bomba borinqueña of Don Rafael Cepeda &
The deceptive revelry of Batucada & Mardi Gras
Ain't no secret,
David Walker, Dandara & Zumbi of Palmares got drunk on my tears
It was my tears,
That quenched the furious thirst of Nat Turner &
Put the power behind all those funny jokes
Comedy? … a costume … a disguise … a clever shield
The acceptable watery mask of Moms Mabley & Richard Pryor
Nzinga's Elixer … a transplanted medicine
A metaphysical ladder … these tears lifted our Souls
Lubricated the throats of Marcus Garvey & Fannie Lou Hamer
Energized the creative will of Arturo Schomberg &
The Schomberg Museum grew up from the hard earned root
On the foundation of historical bricks formed by years of tears
Nzinga's Elixer … our tears … our sacred tears
Where ever we go, we have taken you with us
Each & every day,
Every stitch of my clothes is wet with my crying for you
You are our Soul Food … the key to our mystique
You are our fuel!!!
Africa,
You have covered the whole world swimming in our tears
Singing & dancing & praying & laughing … in our tears
But I wonder,
Mama Africa
Do you ever … have you ever … will you ever
Cry for us???????

ELS ©'10

IN LINDA'S HOUSE
WORLD OF OUR QUEEN MOTHER
FIRST LADY OF THE HOUSE OF UGMA

Pianist / Composer/Arranger /Community Activist Horace Tapscott was an undeniably brilliant catalyst for change & an innovator of the highest order. Tapscott was an ingenious musical magnet, but Linda Hill was not only his main disciple, she was his right arm & his friend. She was always "the" one who was always there & "the" organizer behind the Organization. Tapscott said she was the most talented woman he ever knew & called her Lino. I say, she was an unavoidable power source & an off-the-Richter-scale Piano player's Pianist. Linda was a strikingly beautiful, big boned, dashiki wearing, head as bald as a baby's behind example of African American pride. I always remember her wearing the biggest hoop earrings I had ever seen. Linda scared most folks to death ... she introduced us to the true interdependence of life!

Linda was a for real Amazon. She was also a no nonsense, straight shooter & an unassuming motivator. It all began in her small apartment. Her place was so full of Music & big dreams that we never thought of it as just an apartment. It was the center of existence. It was our umbilical cord. Home was always "Lino's Pad." And it was her house & her dedicated quiet brilliance that was the true glue that held us all together. And believe me when I tell you she was no ordinary glue ... she was a one-of-a-kind type of Sistah. She was a professional Nurse & a full-time Mother & that background manifested itself in every move she made. Even though she was not much older than most of us & a lot younger than some of the others, she was our Mama!!!

Linda was stronger than metal & as soft as was necessary whenever it was necessary to be soft. The woman was tough! She had to be or we would have never survived, because we were one strange unlikely group of characters ... a whole lot of "anything you wanna." We came to L.A. from everywhere & every thing. We were high class, middle class & a whole lot of no class. Music, the Word, the Dance, our Art was our religion & the sacredness of sound was our only common denominator.

And Music ... our Music was everywhere. Music bounced off our every thought & action. We played Music before we ate, while we were eating & then had to have some more Music for dessert. Music was our one & only reason for being alive. It crawled all over the ceiling & was the floor we walked on. It lived in between every board of the floor. Came in out of every corner. Rolled in melodically off the roof top & drifted like a magical spell out of every window. Linda's house was alive with our Music & we lived to immerse ourselves in its beauty. A beauty full of the mysterious unfolding enchantment of the rebirth of ourselves.

We were obsessed ... a wild bunch of creative fanatics. We had been deliberately hand picked ... a select crew of chosen people. Some were chosen by fate ... some by Horace ... others by Linda & eventually by other Musicians. There were so many great Artists that came through UGMA it would take forever to mention them all. But a few of my favorites were Leroy Brooks-Drums, "Black Arthur" Blythe-Alto Saxophone, Jayne Cortez-Poet, Adele Sebastian-Flute, Red Calendar-Bass & Tuba, brothers Butch Morris-Cornet & Wilbur Morris-Bass, Bobby Bradford-Trumpet & Cornet, Ray Draper-Tuba, John Heard-Bass, Rickey Kelly-Vibes, James Newton-Flute, E.W. Wainwright Jr.-Drums & Multi Percussion, John Carter-Alto Sax & Clarinet, Azar Lawrence-Saxophones, Lester Robertson-Trombone, Michael Session-Saxes, David Murray-Tenor Sax & Bass Clarinet, Percy Smith-Artist, Ojenke-Poet, & Everett Brown Jr.-Drums. I was brought into the family on the sly by my friend & brother Drummer Bill Madison. I can still see & hear us when we had two Guitars, three Basses, two full sets of Drums, a couple of Pianists, a Tuba, a Flute, a Singer, a Dancer & several Saxophones & Trumpets on stage at the same time playing our hearts out. Arrangements straight out of Heaven. Sounding tight, like we were one instrument. We were no joke!!! We were a whole brand new breed ... running away from the massive, but lucrative boredom of the Los Angeles studio trivia & a racist Musicians Union. Some of us were "hope to die" traditionalists taking that tradition to a whole new level. Others were coming straight out of the Avant-Garde & played unconventional Musical Masterpieces on traditional & not-so-traditional instruments. All of us were rebels in search of our own voices.

We took our Music out into the Streets, the Parks, into Public Schools, Libraries, Community Centers & Churches. We played everywhere the people were, including innumerable Festivals & Night Clubs, but we always came back home. Home was where the action was! We made Music every single day non-stop on soda bottles, played intricate polyrhythms on Linda's kitchen pots, Pablum boxes & anything else we could get our hands on. And Music bounced off everything, crawled up out of the alley in back of her house & fell out of the sky like comets & shooting Stars. And like clockwork, amazing tunes came racing out of the uncharted universe of our imaginations. Music was the language of our Souls, the blood in our veins. Our Music was a life force all its own. And Linda's house was the center of our existence ... the home of The Pan Afrikan People's Arkestra ... The House of UGMA (The Underground Musicians' Association). Linda's place was the nursery that gave birth to it all. And even when we outgrew the confines of Linda's small South Central apartment &

moved over to Percy's wonderful large house on Figueroa, Linda came & remained our Matriarch.

Everyone talks (and rightfully so) about Horace Tapscott & the UGMA, but none of it would have happened without Linda. Linda ... a big, beautiful dark chocolate Piano-playing, singing, giant of a woman. Linda ... Linda Hill ... Linda the High Priestess of The Pan Afrikan People's Arkestra & UGMA. Linda ... an ebony Queen, who opened her heart, soul & home to a musical movement. A woman who's faith, love & home gave us a home & helped create a dynasty, an unstoppable wave of brave new school Musicians. Yes, it was the strength of Horace's dream. The magical pull of Papa Horace ... he was the magnet that pulled us in. But it was the Music & the organizational magnitude of our Matriarch Linda that was the loving glue that held us together & kept us whole.

Thank you will never be enough. I'm still just another hard-working Artist ... a Musical Poet. Just another number in a long parade of the multitude she helped to create. I have nothing to give to repay the debt for all she gave, but the gift of this short story. It's my way of making sure the world will never forget her & her contributions to the history of this great American Art Form called Jazz. It was from the womb of her house that musical history was disemboweled & reformed & traditional miracles bathed in pride were reclaimed & reborn.

The healing powers of Music ran all over the ceiling of Linda's house like it ran all over our lives & was poured into our hearts with every sound from the streets that brought us to her door.

And a brand new seriously dedicated army of Music Makers was forever changed.

ELS © '10

THERE'S SOMETHING MISSING
or
AIDS: THE THIEF THAT MAKES OUR ANCESTORS CRY
(FOR JAY JOHNSON, ED MOCK, FRANKIE RODRIGUEZ, SYLVESTER, MARGARITA BENITEZ, ALVIN AILEY, FELA ANIKULAPO-KUTI, ERIC "EAZY-E" WRIGHT & CLARENCE GATSON & CAROLYN & WAYNE CORBETT & SYLVIA & MARLON RIGGS & PETER BARCLAY & TOMMY FABIO & ROY HUNDLEY
& the list goes on & on & on & on)

The Ancestors are crying
Their children are dying
There are spaces on the stages where they danced
All strong & handsome
Brilliant & shining
And covered with hard-earned sweat
A sensual warm sweat
Caressing the heat of their bodies
Streams of swirling hot sweat
Blinding sweat
Clinging ..... wet ..... holding on
Like all those audiences held on
to their every move
Moves that stopped time in it's tracks
Moves that took our breath away
And left us all speechless

The Ancestors are crying
Their children are dying
Every time I walk into a Church
I get flashbacks of you ..... Sylvester
Sylvester ..... the world's greatest Gospel Singer
That the world of Gospel
never even got a chance to know
You had to be
The most beautiful teenage boy on planet Earth
You were not handsome
You were stunning ..... beautiful
Boy, you were radiant ..... natural
You ..... were pretty!!!
The first sight of you completely blew me away
And the very first time I heard you sing, mmmmm mmm mm
I knew I must have died & gone to heaven
And even though,
The Church was not ready for you
You were ready

85

And strong enough & wise enough
To take your gift
Out into a more appreciative world, and
There was a whole world
Ready to love you for who you were
But me?
I still see that beautiful little boy
That pretty young boy
I still feel you at every Gospel concert
You're there.....
Somewhere right behind all those Gospel Choirs
Who wouldn't put you out in front

The Ancestors are crying
Their children are dying
Wheelin'
Dealin'
Gang bangin'
Slangin'
Strapped
Pockets fat
Living life on the wild side
Tangling over turf
Just to prove what you're worth
Taking young lives
To earn imaginary "Stripes"
Hope's just a joke
When you're Black & you're broke
And the only way through the maze
Is to rob & sell Dope
Gets to be
Too many dead Homiez & too many tears
Feeling old ..... getting tired
Too many wasted years
Swimming through streets all covered with blood
A heavy cross to bear
To learn to care, to cry, to love
Still, like blades of grass a few come up
Break right through the concrete
Refuse to be just another stone
To be kicked 'round like trash in the street
And nothing can stop a diamond from shining
Once it realizes its own worth
Rapper, Producer, Hip Hop super star
Eazy-E was more than just a Warrior

More at home behind the scenes
Than behind a microphone
Young & sprung
On the technology of the Recording Industry
And always
Aware of the danger in a Ghetto ignored
Cause the streets talk real loud in Compton
He knew, he'd been there
"For The Love Of Money"
"Mama Don't!"
"Daddy Rich"
Made it his mission to reach out & teach
Made it his mission
To record the truth of the youth
To let the youth teach the youth
About the pitfalls & traps of Heroin & Crack
Unsafe sex & child abuse
Hypocrisy & violence, suicide & greed
Even though he was more famous
For his misdeeds, than his good deeds
Or his technical wizardry
Or his ability to see the real
He showed us
The wealth of creativity growing like pearls
Hidden from sight & right in front of us
In the Projects & on the corners
And in the alleys & all those other places
We conveniently forgot to look
And I hear his stamp
In the voices of so many conscious youth
Who, too, can see themselves
Like that blade of grass
Brave enough to break through the concrete
And reach for the sky
Eazy-E was a Poet
Never interested in hiding behind pretty poems
But I still hear you
I still feel you
& because of you
I have hope!!!

The Ancestors are crying
Their children are dying
Frankie ..... Compai
I hear your voice at every Bembé

Calling in the Ancestors
Reacquainting us with African Deities
Singing songs of praise
Of love & peace & better days
Afro/Latin/Be-bop/Cu-bop
Reminding us of the Africa in us
Proud & uncompromising like Fela
Fela & his phenominal Musical/political/spiritual/Afro Beat
His presence felt everywhere
His influence overwhelming
His "Black Man's Cry" was unavoidable
He put our "Sorrow, Tears & Blood"
Out front for everyone to see
The man was always as inspiring
As he was disturbing
Always controversial, but never commercial
He was the "Black President"
The "Chief Priest Of The Shrine"
Even the translation of his name..... a prophecy
"The One Who Emanates Greatness,
Who Carries Death In His Quiver
And Cannot Be Killed By Human Entity"

The Ancestors are crying
Their children are dying
Cariñosa ..... my Love
You've left what remained of your body
And now there's a big hole in my heart
A great big hole
A hole that feels bigger sometimes
Than the hole in the ozone layer
Or is it just the size of that empty space
That hole ..... A space
Full of unanswered echoes dancing in clave
That keep bouncing around in the emptiness
On your side of the bed we shared

And you are here
I can feel all of you!
Off-stage, on-stage, backstage,
In front of & in back of every curtain
Somewhere real close to every microphone
I see you in the shadows
Of every stage show, in every rehearsal hall,
In every movie theater

On every single dance floor
There are spaces
Empty spaces full of even more emptiness
Sacred spaces
Spaces once so full of a beauty so powerful
Your beauty
Your show-stopping beauty
Once so full of life, it left us all speechless
There are spaces
Spaces full of emptiness
Holy spaces
Spaces once so full of you
The beauty of you
The passionate power of you
A beauty so strong even death cannot steal it
Cannot stop it ..... will not stop it!!!
And even now in your absence
We're left speechless
Only this time we've been silenced
By exhaustion, ignorance & fear
Petrified by fear ..... overwhelmed by fear Terrified!!!
We've been brought to a standstill
Terrified by the unavailability
Of an indifferent medical establishment
Just another disinterested business
Always more interested in financial status
Than in the status of one's health
And we stand here
Too afraid to open our mouths
Don't want to stir up too much of a fuss, or
The thief might get hungry & come looking for us

The Ancestors are crying
Their children are dying
Your bodies have left us & we feel deserted
Were you really just tired?
Tired of fighting AIDS & public opinion
And insurance companies?
Or was it really
The racism, the sexism, the cold uncaring stares?
Or was it
The greedy ... money-loving profiteers
That you were tired of?
Or were you just sick & tired
Or were you just tired of being sick

Tired of being sick & tired of waiting on us
Waiting
        & waiting
                & waiting
                        & waiting
Waiting for us to open our eyes & do something
Anything!!!!!!!
It's time for us to stop running on fear
Can't you hear?????

Our Ancestors are crying & our children dying!!!
And finally ..... you ..... you are all here
Does it always have to take such strife
For us to listen & admit our kids were right
Cause when the chips are down
There's only one fight ..... and
"We're All In The Same Gang!"

Does anybody even hear our Ancestors tears???
It's time we listen
There's something missing!!!!!

IN THE NIGHT
(WHEN ALL YOU CAN SAY IS MMMMM!!!)

Asleep?
Alone in bed
The night
Was not about to let me sleep
You know,
It even had the nerve
To slap me awake
Bold
Like an earthquake
Powerful!!
No shy entrance, this night
No manners at all

And like a Cheshire cat
I cursed the night
For putting an end
To all my "let's pretend"
For setting free my ability to smile
For waking up my half-dead hormones
With shocks of craving
The night drowned all my never agains
All my cool
Being blown away
As easily
As a feather in a hurricane

Asleep??
Alone??
The night won't let me sleep
Desire running wild
On fire
Burning with distractions of too many memories
Of that once in a lifetime morning
Filled with rejuvenating tantric magic
& music & you
& talk & you
The absolute sweaty sweetness
Of being wrapped in a blanket of you

Mmmmm.....
Who wants to sleep anyway???

Be a fool to try ... don't even stand a chance
Swimming in the middle of a nocturnal river
Swept away by wave after wave after wave
Of clouds dripping dark chocolate memories
Sleep?????
Sleep just can't compete with a taste of you &
All I can say is ... *Mmmmmmm!!!*

THIS SISTER AIN'T QUITTING!!!
OR LIFE DODGIN' THE MARGIN OF ACCEPTABLE RISK

Been living my life on borrowed time
Going to sleep exhausted & I still wake up feeling tired
Beat up & almost knocked down from doing the MS* shuffle
Got tossed around, tricked, caught up & sucked into
What could be my own demise, disguised by
An innocent looking smile on the iron jaws of science
(And any fool knows that science never lies)

But one taste of truth
Forced me to look at their toxic delusions & BLAAAM!!!
I opened my mouth & saw the fake beauty of
All that Mercury staring back at me
Sitting there ... just as cold & bold as it wanted to be
An enemy had moved in & made itself at home in my teeth
I was caught, entrapped by a medical fantasy, a Venus Flytrap &
Now all "their" pretty mercury's really got a hold on me

Even after all my shuckin' & jiving & ducking & denying &
Trying' to make every kind of outlandish bargain with God
There's still no place I can hide, 'cause
I'm still waking up tired & still finding myself riding
In the Margin of "their" Acceptable Risk
Acceptable? ... By who's definition?
Marginal? ... Compared to what?
Me? ... Are "they" really talking about me? ... Not this Sister!!!
Uh, Ugh! ... Can't be! ... Not me! ... But who?
Watch your back, cause there's always some mad scientist
Cooking up some new strange brew in his cauldron of doom &
Dr. Strangelove wants to try it all out on you

"Oh no, can't be!" ... "Not here in the land of the free!"
"That kind of stuff just doesn't happen today! But.......?"
Dodging the Margin is acceptable ... to who???
When science is God, the margin gets hazy
It's a racket ... A scam! ... It's a multi-million dollar game
The whole concept is inhumane, it's madness, completely insane
It's crazy!!!

"The Margin of Acceptable Risk"
Is anywhere the powers that be, want it to be &
They want "it" anywhere there's a profit to be made, it's all about

Money, money, money all the way to the grave
Like the so called benevolent syphilis experiment in Tuskegee
Only this time "their" experiment is me &
It's as moveable & obscene as a corporate baron's morality &
As clean as the untested "miracle of "their" Estrogen dreams
As unasked for & unnecessary as the cruel gift of Agent Orange &
As evil as dumping on unsuspecting Farmworkers
Sitting like ducks, stuck, getting sprayed picking crops
This is a nightmare in real time!!!
And unfortunately, this time it's my time

The "Margin" is a very profitable lie ... it's as sick, as sick can go
Look at me, I'm living proof, all this drama ain't no joke
It's anything "the scientific community" claims it to be &
It's whatever "they" claim it to be & as long as it's done for
"Their" financial gain, in the name of "their" progress &
The only real casualties are you, our neighbors & friends & me
Seems to be, The Margin of Acceptable Risk is
Whatever "they" can get away with & "they" get away with it
All the time!!!!!!!

So here I be ... still tired ... almost whipped
Caught up & all wrapped up
Locked in the temple of some invisible "madman's" technology
Just one more insignificant waste of "their" corporate space,
Another loud mouth expendable Artist
A "marginal" target sitting in the center of "their" bullseye
But, I refuse to go out living my life like some sacrificial lamb
In The Margin of "their" Acceptable Risk
Just a new age human receptacle, a toxic waste dump on legs
Hidden away in some unethical, but scientifically acceptable deception

I don't know what "they" been smokin, but my life ain't no joke &
As long as there's one of us strong enough to write this Poem,
I'm gonna be a thorn in all "their" self-righteous myths
This Sister wasn't born to quit & even though
I still wake up tired & MS may steal some of my fire,
I plan to live my life right up 'til the day that I die & I know
MS may eventually get the best of me, but until
The White Citizen's Council unanimously elects
A Blue/Black man Imperial Grand Dragon of the Ku Klux Klan
The Margin of Acceptable Risk will continue to be
Completely unacceptable!!!!!!!

MEMORIES IN THE MANY KEYS OF HORIUCHI
INSPIRED BY GLENN ATSUSHI HORIUCHI 3/7/1955 - 6/3/2000

They named him Glenn Atsushi
A not so quiet Baby boy
Born into a world clouded by way out of focus uncomfortable secrets
Another muffled voice in a universe of ever present whispers
A small bundle surrounded by walls full of unspoken memories
& he grew
Listening to those whispers ... whispers of an invisible history
A mystery ... a hole in time that needed to be filled
& he grew
A rebellious wild child
Swimming through a deluge of Elementary School wiseguys
Playing hopscotch dodging verbal violence
A little boy bruised by little foul mouthed fools, but
All the racial isolation & complications & frustrations of childhood Asthma
Just gave him the space to meditate
A time to quietly turn his rage into a reservoir of fuel
A tool to open one of many doors on the long road to a beckoning destiny
& he grew
He ... thirsty/dehydrated like a long ignored sponge ... he
Just another child lost in a desert of acceptable invisibility
Boy greedily drank in everything
He drank in all the joy & pain
The strength & beauty & all the shame
& somewhere
In between the proud passionate Shakuhachi of his Grandfather
& the pretty complexities of Beethoven
He met the arrogant all up in your face boldness of the Blues
& the Blues introduced him to the slick hipness of "Bird"
& Charlie "Yardbird" Parker's musical gymnastics
Led him to the other worldliness of John Coltrane
& "Trane" took him all the way "out"
Took him "out" into the world beyond Bebop
& all those walls built on decades of shame came tumbling down
& he grew
The Spirit of creativity had been waiting
The gate was finally open
& the memories came down like a flood
When that last dam broke the model Minority drowned
& Glenn came out running like a man possessed
Jumped out of the blandness of the shadows of mediocrity
& slapped down a lifetime of hypocrisy
He came out screaming ... a Sansei Jazzman preaching

Like a man playing Taiko rhythms on piano keys
Stomping all over stereotypes
Kicking awake all the memories that history had tried to erase &
Memories of the Issei Spirit came climbing up out of basements
Memories of Lindy Hopping Nissei came dancing down from attics
Sassy Jazz bands & undefeatable Manzanar Voices came out
Swinging, BeBoping & knocking open a thousand or more closet doors
It was Horiuchi time
& he grew
Glenn was an insatiable musical tiger
Wilder than any lion & as unpredictable as a monsoon
But then ... without a moment's notice
He'd turn it all around & be so unbelievably gentle
You could even hear the sound
Of a snowflake falling way up on the top of Mount Fuji
His Music a melodic Poetry ... a Horiuchi fire
Akido in Jazztime ... the Brother's music was strong
Strong enough to open doors & make folks want to right the wrongs
Glenn was a major nail in the coffin of "the passive Asian"
The reincarnation of a lot of what the world wanted forgotten
But instead of being whipped into silence ... he grew
A lean wiry guy, skinny as a rail, but
He defied size & became an unstoppable giant
A strange mix of music, science, math & spirit
A pragmatic mystic
The man was an irrepressible giant of a Spirit
With Ancient battle weary eyes
Tired eyes full of memories & hard-won victories
Wise eyes that helped us see the real
And now???
Somewhere on this crazy little piece of rock we call planet Earth
(maybe right this second)
There's another not so quiet baby being born
A beautiful, brilliant, artistic wild child
A rebellious child surrounded by unmentionable mysteries
A Spirit obsessed with the dignity & freedom of all humanity
I will see you Glenn in their eyes
Those same Ancient battle-weary eyes
Old passionate eyes still ready to undress the same old lies
You can try to hide, but
I will know you by the conscious drama in the songs they sing
I will feel your presence in
The gentler side of power & the wilder side of gentleness
Of the next generation &
I will recognize the Asian splendor of you in them &

Hear you in the percussive pianistic gymnastics
That they think is new, but I'll know it's you &
I will find you alive in the mind of the child
That refuses to accept anything less than total respect
Some Spirits are too obsessed with change to stay away &
I've got to say thanks, my Friend, for bringing us into your world
I hope you knew you'll always have a home in mine!!!

A LOVE STORY

This is not just another love story, but it is a love story. This is a story about the love of Nature, the respect of nature & those who only see it as another exploitable commodity. A not-so-tall tale about the "not so kind" kind of people who find it impossible to do either. About people who have traded their Souls for the lust of power & the love of the dollar has completely gotten in the way of every remnant of common sense & simple courtesy. This story was written for those who've lost their way. This is a tale for those who've forgotten that the desecration of the Sacred is not a joke. Mother Nature stops laughing when She's misused & taken for granted. This is not another love story, but a story to remind the mindless that Nature doesn't play!

This story was written for those whose self-righteously pompous, condescending Fathers take pleasure in the murder of innocence & learn morality from their prissy, insecure, vindictive Mothers. And for all those who nursed at the breasts of overworked & underfed slaves & got fat on milk which belonged to another's lonely, milk-starved Babies. And grew up & forgot the source of the life force that made them strong. This was written for those who respect nothing they can not spend, sell, trade or buy. And this is for those who chop down the rain forests, or any other kind of forest, in order to build concrete/steel/aluminum/glass/plastic Ecology Centers. Then have the audacity to ask, "where have all the flowers gone?"

It was written for those who wear clothing woven from cotton threads (dripping with blood of slave labor & the pain of Campesino sweat.) For those who are serious about nothing … nothing, but their own uncomfortable version of comfort. And for those who love nothing they have not first corrupted &/or destroyed, or hidden behind nondescript fences all in the name of being better than, stronger than, smarter than. The latest edition in a long line of those afflicted with dangerous delusions of grandeur. Another smug new age Don Quixote, forever trying to fulfill some grim fantasy quest, still on the road chasing unattainable dreams of becoming invincible.

This story is a reminder for those who mind rape their own Mothers, exploit their own Sisters' half-naked bodies to sell gas-guzzling, air-polluting, luxurious cars that destroy the environment & then accuse the rest of us of obscenity. And for those who blindly worship Youth, disrespect their Elders & treat their darling Children like brainless pets. And then spend millions of dollars trying to psychoanalyze away the problems they worked so hard to create. And with crocodile tears in their eyes try to understand all the reasons why their once sweet Children are running "buck wild" in the streets, glorifying the sexist Poetics of Gangster Rap instead of listening to them.

This is for those who think progress is burning down fruit trees so they can build Coca-Cola factories & Fast Food Monster Burger Complexes. For those who give Folks all the whiskey they can drink & then call them prideless drunkards when they are misled enough to drink it. For those who knowingly destroy priceless land so they can build Playgrounds & Parking Lots for their precious Children who no longer respect them. Children who will do any thing & everything to be anything as long as it's not "them." Not to mention the self-proclaimed "Upper Crust" … the so-called "Hunting Class." Those "High Society" folks who indiscriminately kill animals. Not for food, clothing or shelter, but for kicks (because they can think of no other form of exciting entertainment.) And for those who've lost contact with all that is sacred & sensual & have turned the Art of Dancing into a public orgy, because they can no longer function & "get it on" in private.

Isn't it amazing how those who don't know how to live respectfully with Nature & joyfully for Her Children always find themselves rejected by Nature & Her Children & then don't ever seem to understand why. It never ceases to blow my mind every time one of those who dare to try to destroy Mother Nature are caught off guard & completely surprised when She comes up mad & turns the world upside down to defend Herself. For it's only the wise who are humble before the Elements that come to realize the strength in their humility is the only way to reap a sustainable, healthy harvest. This is a Prayer for the restoration of the humanity of the inhumane who are still drunk on all the skullduggery* of their own inhumanity.

This is not just another love story, but it is a love story. Because somehow, we're going to have to find enough love within ourselves to have more than a little bit of pity. Pity for those, who in their greedy arrogance, have the nerve to attempt to own the flowers, the trees, the water & all the animals. Pity because they want it all. They think they need it all so they can completely control the universe, the Moon & even the air we breathe. But no matter what, it will never be enough! Pity them & their blind megalomania … they're just another very expensive cover. Shallow & transparent … because it only helps to expose their cowardice, their weakness. For only an absolute coward has to control everything. They are afraid!!! They are an out-of-control, insecure, naked fear on the loose & their pitiful fear of the unknown is so great it makes even the Stars cry.

Pity the fool! Because anyone who has lost all semblance of manners & is foolish enough to think they're big enough to try to hold Mother Earth tightly in their hands like a cheap toy, has lost their right to cry….. Or be the least bit shocked when She gets tired of playing the same old shameful games & with an uncontainable vengeance eats all off all of their fingers, devours their greed & swallows their young! Nature can be a very dangerous Mother when she loses her sense of humor.

No, this is not just another love story, but it is a very painful real story. An unbelievably frustrating, but hopeful love story. And for those of us who still live to smell the flowers.....

This story is our story!

IN THE GARDEN OF ECSTASY

Ecstasy
is
A forest of Guitars
Dancing thru Rainbows
with
Nights full of typewriters
&
Days that taste like Piña
Ecstasy
is
An ocean of Clarinets
playing
Jazz & Street Music
Harlem Mambo Music
A rainbow of Music
A shower of Flute Songs
whose
only meaningful job
is
Purifying the path
to
Ecstasy

PLATINUM COATED DREAMS
CARBON COPY SCHEMES

Rip off the neighborhood Good Will Store??? We got to be completely out of the little bit that's left of our minds! Talk about stupid. Ripping off a local joint in the same 'Hood" we grew up in, a few blocks from my Mama's house? A local second-hand shop with a whole lot of nothing. A place running on empty that got damn near nothing to take. Another one of Loco Willy Lee's tired "pipe dream" schemes & we fell for it... AGAIN!!!

Dumb! Dumb!! Dumb!!! Nothing about this dumb nonsense makes any kind of real sense. I just don't get it, or maybe I just don't want to get it!

How are we supposed to do this shit? Jake is "high" as a kite. So "wasted," ain't no telling what he's gonna do. He's just as likely to shoot somebody, as to "nod out." Fading, drifting, like a slow motion cartoon gliding through the slime into the twisted blissful twilight zone of Heroin heaven. Sonia? Sis "got down" on one of her double doses of "Crystal Meth" courage. Girl's all amped up, wired to the gills on "Speed" & just won't shut up. Keeps running off at the lips about how she's got to rob & steal just to put some food in her non-existent baby's mouth. And then there's me... Go for anything me!!! A washed up Wannabe stuck on stupid me... so scared I'm about to pee on myself!

All of us, staring at some poor jerk of a clerk who's just trying to hold on to his façade of a job. A square, scared, minimum-wage-earning sucker who couldn't care less about the Good Will or us. A poor, terrified, hard-working S.O.B. who's probably wondering "how low would we really go for a little piece of chump change?"

How low could we go??? Us? Ain't no telling. Your guess is as good as mine. You never know, when you're working with four nickel plated fools who are more than willing to throw away all their freedom & risk everybody's lives (including their own)... all for a little bit of money!!!!!!!

ELS © '90

A BITTER FERTILIZER

(INSPIRED & DEDICATED TO
THE MANY INCARNATIONS OF MICHAEL MARCUM
MICHAEL THE BOY, PRISON INMATE MARCUM B5437,
& MICHAEL MARCUM
ASST. SHERIFF OF SAN FRANCISCO 1993 – 2004)

His Daddy was a good-looking man
A volatile, violent, some time sweet-talking man
Scared ... beating & punching & kicking his way
        through a cold-blooded world
Getting even
A scared, scary, angry man
All the way drunk to the bone on his own violence
Brutality had him stuck in a viclous maze
Crazed ... an inescapably lost man
Who, himself as a kid, had been whipped into submission
And schooled well into the sadistic tradition
Of sugar-coated bruises
Followed by bouquets of beautiful flowers
Mirages to camouflage the cruel

And wild, passionate, romantic nights
Full of the same old pretty lies
Until the next time
And there was always a next time &
A next time & a next time & a next time
Until one of those many times
When life called him on the emptiness of all his pretty words
But even thinking about calling him on any of his shit
Was like pushing all the right buttons to the wrong switch
The switch that turned on every trigger
Desperate triggers
Triggers that were tightly wrapped
Around an always ready insecure short fuse
A quick to hit ... an unapologetic heavy hand
Man was an open wound
An unfillable hole that only ran hot & cold
An out of control bomb on legs
Looking for any excuse to explode

This guy ... his Daddy ... was "the Man"!
A chilling fact that he never let anyone forget
In his house ... he was the only rule
The ultimate King of fear
And almost every time he was at home ... peace split!!!

Quickly slipped out through the cracks
Ran away & disappeared & even the earth
Beneath every pair of feet
In every inch of the place he lived in trembled
And one more little boy began to die
And he continued to die
And he died & he died & he died
Every single time, he had to try to cover his ears, or hide,
Or be quiet, or silently sit there
Listening … drowning in all that terror
Never ever any time just to be a little child

Boy was born dying ... Kid was a little old man
Growing a little bit colder each & every day
Growing colder
Older & colder each & every day
Every day growing & growing crazy with rage
Helplessly cringing … a little boy listening
Waiting & listening & listening & waiting &
Waiting & waiting & waiting
And listening to his Mama cry, over & over & over again

BANG!!!!!!
Bye bye!
And then the Cops came
The Force in Blue moved brutally in
With the well-rehearsed grace of
A choreographed invasion of uncaring witnesses
Caused the sudden unwanted premature birth
Of an unpredictable creation
And a brand new nightmare began
It was frightening
As a large part of another Manchild's soul just walked away

CLANG!!!!!!!!
The sound of the gates of hell
That sound ... the finality of that unholy sound
Those unbelievably eerie sounding gates
Diabolically designed
To murder whatever pride was still alive
CLANG!!!!!!!!
Dazed & in a state of shock
Emotionally barren ... feelings gone
Like a zombie, emotionally deaf, dumb & blind
Stripped of everything

Physically & spiritually naked
Degraded, insulted, humiliated, demoralized, dehumanized
Voices of sick suckers yelling ... "Get used to it!"
"This is your new home ... Boy!!!"
This was his first day "Inside the Walls"
His introduction to the land of the living dead

CLANG!!!!!!!!
Welcome to hell!
Welcome to the world of hurt boys & wounded men
An army of men
Whose souls were destroyed when they were boys
A sad army of grown-up boys, some so completely destroyed
Prison was the only dependable,
Secure home they'd ever really known
Some so destroyed ... they could only feel joy
When they destroyed the souls of other men
Who had been destroyed when they were boys

Prison is another world
A University & a garden
A garden full of the kind of weeds
That are guaranteed to come alive
Any place where the Sun is not allowed to shine
A garden ... perfumed by the aromatic stench
Of ten thousand farts & the musty smell of too many
Sweaty men & the ever-present
Rancid scent of resentment & dread
A never quiet garden, serenaded by nights crowded with
A wacked out, hair raising, irritating choir of hundreds of
Exhausted, angry, halfway sleeping, snoring men
Death threats, a constant barrage of
Foul language & murders & rapes
Blood-curdling screams &
The warning sounds of a Guard's jingling keys

Prison is a university
A school for Jailhouse Lawyers
Who will save your life for a price &
Slicker-than-slick Prison poster-boy pimps ... getting rich
Running major Gender-bending prostitution scams
A school where you too can come to master
The international Prison art of learning
To always sleep on your back with your eyes wide open
Prison is a university of the absurd

And the main Courses are "Staying Alive 101"
And learning how to survive living beside
The same kind of hateful folks who drive the best of folks
To commit the worst of crimes

CLANG!!!!!!!!
Getting out of Prison is the easy part
It's getting the Prison out of you that's hard to do
Like leaving the comfort of
The monotonous ritual of the predictable &
Not only escaping enemies, but
All the guilt you feel ... leaving, walking away from friends
Real true blue no nonsense friends
Friends, War Buddies, Brothers
Men who had walked through the storm together
Friends who would think nothing
Of giving up their lives just to save yours

Now you're just one more lost guy
Trying to find his way home
Wandering along a strange & dangerous shore
Like a fish out of water
Sort of hard to know how to navigate in unknown territory
Like walking out of a garden
Of poisonous snakes & beautiful wild flowers
It's scary,
Almost like leaving a familiar jungle
And diving into the heart of a whirlpool &
Learning all over again that silence is not always deadly &
That it's all right
To close your eyes in the night & just go to sleep And dream
Safe & comfortable
Smiling & dancing a brand new dance
You got a chance!

CLANG!!!!!!!!
And then you wake up ... shaken
Maybe you had to pinch yourself the first time
Before you realized
This shit is real ... it's not a dream
You're really alive & you're really outside &
Something unbelievable
A miracle bigger than all the ugliness
Of Prison life has just transpired
And that miracle is you!

That miracle is knowing
It's not over & there's so much stuff to do

That miracle came in accepting
That it was Kismet that dictated the map
That it was your fate & your faith
That carved out that inescapable path
Wouldn't let you get away & let you know
That to save your Soul & rescue the Souls of
All those men like your Father
You were going to have to drag all of us
Back into the hell of that world
That world of hurt boys
A new breed of seriously cold, furious hurt boys
Angry hurt boys
Destined to become the next generation of wounded men

You knew it would not be easy, but
You were on a mission to convince anyone who would listen
And you succeeded … you let the entire planet know
It's a whole lot cheaper
To put safety valves on the pressure cookers
Than to sit around waiting
For them to blow up all over the place & then
Moaning & groaning & $pending
The rest of every single Tax payer's life
Paying the expensive price of
Cleaning up the unnecessary wreckage
When the minimal expense of Education & Art
In-house Drug Programs & Anti-Violence Programs
Ain't no big thing!

Call it damage control!! … Call it good sense!
Call it Preventive Medicine!!!
You showed us the truth &
The alternatives are too horrible to imagine
Functional illiteracy & stifled creativity &
Addictions to violence & drugs
Are some of the most lonely, humiliating,
Dangerous & costly kinds of poverty &
"He who takes away expression,
Gives birth to unspeakable negativity"

So I, for one, want to thank you
For having the guts to keep it real

For showing us another way
Prison is a University of the absurd
A garden of extremes
But you broke your own chains
Turned it all around & allowed the walking wounded
To see all kinds of alternative possibilities
Your example gave so many others a chance
A chance to swim in the sea of life toward real freedom

And truth is I would not wish that brutal & heartless world
On you or anyone else, but it took every bit
Of that horror & madness to create what you've created
It took every little bit
Of that foul & painfully bitter fertilizer
For the garden to grow
To produce the miraculous crop
That only you could have produced
Prison may be another world
A powerful, destructive world, but this time it's produced
A positive, beautiful miracle far bigger than itself
And Michael ... this time that miracle is you

OMBLIGAO EN ARGENTINA
(RECORDANDO LA MAJESTAD DE TANGO)

Yo recuerdo la danza mistica y la musica sensual
Y el sabor a cuerpos sudorosos
El ambiente de nuestro orgullo arrogante
Creatividad completa desenfrenada
Fuímos Guapachosos bailadores negros
Celebrandonos en Templos del solar
Yo
Recordando los días
Días extáticos bailando contigo
Libre, auténtica y una esclava de nadie
Tú y yo
Una pareja conectada eternamente
Bailando ombligao
Un exorcismo a pesar de una sombra de la esclavitud
Colmada de una libertad inconquistada
Bailando adueñarse de fiebre apasionada
Frenéticamente, pero suave y sin vergüenza

Recordando estos días lejanos
Como un torrente de memorias
Y una cascada de la verdad
Memorias
Rompiendo el silencio de mentiras históricas
Días inovidables que me persiguen
Repercuciónes de tristezas dolorosas
Recuerdo los días ensangretados
Y las noches africando en santuarios secretos
Felicidad clandestina, una alegría prohibida
Bailando ombligao
Bailando en refugios cubierto de lágrimas
Yo recuerdo
La suciedad de nuestras pistas de baile
Y el precio pagado pál derecho de danzar

Recuerdo la magia de noches estrelladas
Noches borrachadas de la danza
Memorias sagradas de un legado inolvidable
Tú y yo, dos volcánes ritmicos
Dos rebeldes prietos
Dos espíritus negros mas viejo del tiempo
Bailando ombligao

Nuestro ritual santificado contra La Regla de malvados
Y te recuerdo
Tú y estos días
Bailando como locos en los callejonés
Discípulos atrevidos de la iglesia de bailando ombligao
A pesar de la fantasma endiablada de la esclavitud
Bailando contigo y tú espíritu inmortal
Tú y yo … fuimos uno
Un cuerpo, un corazón, un alma inseparable
Tú y yo … purificandonos en la luna
Una pareja inconquistada
Juntos en espíritu pá siempre jamás
Bailando
Bailando ombligao
En Argentina

NAVEL TO NAVEL IN ARGENTINA
(REMEMBERING THE MAJESTY OF TANGO)

I remember the sensual Music & mystical Dancing
Air so full of sweaty bodies you could taste it
The atmosphere saturated with our arrogant pride
A totally wild creativity
We were beautiful Black dancers
Celebrating ourselves
In self-proclaimed temples anywhere
Me
Remembering those days
Ecstatic days dancing with you
Pure, free & a slave of nobody
You & I
Soul-mates connected by eternity
Dancing navel to navel
An exorcism in spite of the shadow of slavery
Overflowing with unconquerable freedom
Dancing possessed by the fever of passion
Frantically, but shamelessly smooth

Remembering those far away days
Like a flood of memories
And a waterfall of truth
Memories
Tearing up the silence of historical lies
Unforgettable days that haunt me
Echoes of painful sadnesses
I remember those bloody days
And our Africanizing nights in secret sanctuaries
Undercover happiness, forbidden joy
Dancing navel to navel
Dancing in safe havens covered with tears
I remember
The dusty muddy dirt of our dance floors
And the price we paid for the right to dance

I remember the magic of those nights full of stars
Nights completely drunk on dance
Sacred memories of an unforgettable legacy
You & I, two rhythmic volcanoes
Two dark rebels
Two Black Spirits older than time
Dancing navel to navel

Our holy ritual against the Divine Law of the lawless
And I remember
I remember you & those days
Dancing like we were out of our minds in the alleys
Proud disciples of the church of dancing navel to navel
Right in the face of the evil ghost of slavery
Dancing with you & your bigger-than-life Spirit
You & I ... we were one
One body, one heart, one inseparable Soul
You & I ... bathing in the moonlight
One unconquered couple
Together forever & ever
Dancing
Dancing navel to navel
In Argentina

EASTSIDE VIBES

The Streets used to be alive on the Eastside. I remember when our side of town felt safe & comfortable & the streets were something to be proud of.

Coming home was almost like a free outdoor concert. Streets always on fire with the daily rhythmic ritual of Stickball & the slamming of Dominoes sounded like Claves. There were loud-mouthed, wanna-be Shot Callers & fast-talking Numbers Runners. Congueros & Panderetas playing Rumba & Bomba & Plena everywhere. DooWop came pouring out of Subway Stations & hallways. Big city Blues boldly creeping 'round & wild Mambos & Cha Cha Cha's slid slickly out of your Neighbors' open windows. Non-stop Bochinche rolled off every Stoop & Old Folks added spice to otherwise nondescript afternoons by minding everybody else's business & "talking trash" on all the corners.

It was our world! And in our world you could actually taste the flavor of every bit of our weakness & the all-encompassing creativity in our greatness. The Eastside was our mainline to always & the secure unchanging nature of its existence made those Streets a predictable Dreamland & we knew with every bone in our body that it would last forever!

But we got too comfortable, closed our eyes as it was all falling apart. Our secure world started dying & left a hole in that too busy place that once was our Soul. And it's all gone now. Silence is running around in the nude & holding hands with hopelessness & all hugged up with Booze & drowning in Drugs. These days when the Sun comes up on the Eastside it's as quiet as a Cemetery. Now you can hear a pin drop on the sidewalk & the only music you get to hear is coming out of cars as they go passing by. Ain't nothing happening in the Streets anymore. No Congas, nobody cares about Stickball, or DooWop, or playing The Numbers & there's nothing left to even gossip about.

And then the Sun goes down & the Eastside seems to come alive. The slamming percussion of Dominoes, the rhythmic passion of Panderetas have been replaced by the "RAT A TAT TAT" of automatic weapons & a thunderous lullaby of drive-by shootings. A nocturnal death dance. Like Vampires they come crashing down, or crawling up out of their self-made graves. When the Sun stops shining on the Eastside, it's like nights of the living "Baseheads." Strange folks, folks skinny enough to do Hula Hoops in a Cheerio. Glassy-eyed, gray-skinned, Twiggy-looking folks. Cousins! Like Zombies, they invade the stillness of the night & the air drips death. An army of the living dead on a suicidal mission of self-destruction on the installment plan.

But, uncomfortably, we still return seeking whatever's left of yesterday's dreams. The rhythm of our innocence, the beauty of the melody that was us. Days when we cared enough to be a community & the Conga Drums were the heartbeat of the streets on our side of town.

Uncomfortably, we return to the uncomfortable, trying to re-mind the living they're alive. Like stubborn lyrical phantoms we return. We! Like unstoppable rhythms, we're on a "mission" to rekindle the faith in the part of us that has none.

We come to turn on the fire & breathe the joy of life into the living. A joy we're determined to recapture. We come back to reclaim the joy we allowed to be stolen on the Eastside. We come back to drop the necessary flavor into the pot. We are the missing spice needed to rebuild our lives.

It's gonna take a whole lot of work & it won't be easy. Please come with us. It's going to take all of us, each & every one of us & we have absolutely nothing to lose but our losses!

HASHTAR
(INSPIRED BY THE MUSICAL ARTISTRY OF
OSTAD MAHMOUD ZOUFONOUN)

It had been sitting unseen
Quietly
In dark dusty corners for as long as anybody could remember
An ancient soundless relic
A dried up piece of wood
That some forgotten someone had carved
Into a gigantic wooden spoon
Now relegated to a prankster's joke
A big old four-foot Magic Wand
Devoid of Magic so long
It had forgotten it had ever had a song to sing
What kind of devious mind could even conceive of a singing spoon?
Must have been one of those phony crazy dreamers
Or was it just a daring Artist … or maybe some mad Carver
You know the kind
The kind whose creations
Always fall out of fashion as fast as they come into existence
But there it was, never the less, a carving
A work of Art
That somebody somewhere
Must have thought was something great while creating it
Now thrown aside … forgotten … discarded … ignored
Hidden away in some non descript Flea Market
'Til an annoyed Muse said she wasn't having any fleas in the Market
And to keep the peace, an amused Destiny intervened
Demanded the Site be a flea free zone &
Reclaimed the space as a Persian Playground
An international outdoor Marketplace
An urban haven for homeless artifacts
And a gentle force … moving slowly … cautiously
Weighted by history & wisdom
An ageless Elder
A Sage obsessed with the beauty of harmonic balance
A Wiseman completely drunk on Song was called
Called in by something … a beckoning … a pull that sang to him
Sang to him from some mysterious somewhere
Deep inside that big old wooden spoon
Felt like
Being struck by lightning, a knowing demanding to be known
In a flash, they heard the Magic
They listened … locked in an otherworldly vibration

Knew each other intuitively
Moved into each other immediately
Spoke melodiously to each other
In a language stronger than Song & older than words
An electrical declaration of the inevitable
A spiritual unavoidable flowing … A creative enchantment growing
Growing
Like an uncontrollable fire between them, naturally supernatural
Fate was calling
And the Spirit of a thrown away piece of wood began to dance again
And the Soul of a Master Craftsman in tune with the Cosmos listened
And he knew with everything in him it was singing &
Singing only to him
When he added
Those eight strings & frets & things to that oversized spoon
They merged
The strings … the spoon … the wood … all the Music that was in him
They melted into each other & became something different
Something new
They'd been brought together by the profoundly unfathomable
Moving surely, melodically, they didn't know where
But moving
Always moving … growing … becoming … driven
Being led by the sound of the Bass in their heart
And driven by a borderless passion older than time
Hashtar … Offspring of dreams
The rhythmic key to a miraculous door in the Soul of our ears
Shhhhhhhhh
Can you hear them?

BLUE TO THE BONE
(TRIBUTE TO REGINALD LOCKETT 11/5/47-5/15/08)

Reggie may have been born in a College town, but
Oakland moved herself inside his Soul & it was on
Country slick, tongue in cheek magnificent
A City sophisticate who never scraped the mud off his boots
He was an intellectual Trickster
Directed by the never silent voices of Ancestral Memory
Dined daily on mega-doses of pride
Sprinkled with pain, sautéed in knowledge
Became fruit off the tree of "we're gonna make it"
Reginald Lockett was a straight-shooting,
No nonsense, wise-cracking, flirty kinda guy
A City/Country man who bled that slow, raw, regal
Keep on pushin' power of the Gut-Bucket Blues
You could hear it in every Poem he ever wrote
All Reggie had to do was smile & you felt it
Had a twinkle in his eyes that drew you into
Those makes you wanna "show out" & "act a fool" kind Blues
While on the other side of town
The "high faluting" Literati wearing pity like perfume
Wallowed around in those comfortably fashionable Cafes
Discussing the lives of "poor misunderstood Artistes"
Who'd been dripping abstract angst so long
Their bleeding hearts overflowed all over the place
'Til even the dead knew they were in need of a transfusion or two
Reggie was simply an old school "Race Man"
All his life he worked too hard to whine
Loved him some Esther Philips, Bobby Blue Bland & B.B. King
Reggie'd smirk
And I could taste the Poetic irony in the words they sang
Loved the Music of Words, the rhythms
Of us & himself too much to piss away time
So he worked like a madman at his Craft
Worked with a fanaticism bigger than the Middle Passage
The name of his game was
"Ain't gonna let nobody turn me around" & he did it all for us
In the stench of this whirlpool of Wannabe's
Where a loud mouth &
Demeaning language is all you need to get to a Mic
Reggie was the real deal
No sequins, no frills, no tears, no rants
Just a one hundred percent "Citified" Country guy

Ten steps out of the Juke Joint
And always a few seconds ahead of the Lynch Mob
An intellectual Trickster from beginning to end
Reggie was Oaktown's Soul Man, Blue to the bone
A 12 Bar, dark brown, bitter sweet masterpiece
Our chocolate treasure
Who forced us
To always look beyond "The Ceiling" & keep on climbing
Reginald Lockett was a Blues Poem

YEMAYÁLANDIA
(FOR YEMAYÁ & OLOKUN)

Two moons over the ocean
Waves caressing the waters edge
Night always brings life
To the bottom of the sea
Creatures of darkness dance & sing
To the music of coral & shell fish
& things
The melody of a sea plant being born
An underwater symphony
It's never very quiet
Never very still
Never ..... ever
When night falls at the bottom of the sea

MOTHER NATURE'S REVENGE

She was just a little flower
Never bothered anybody
Just sat there
Minding her own business
Her world was quietly simple
Serene, peaceful
Full of joy
And that's the way it had always been

She was just a little flower
Silently sitting on her hillside
Surrounded by the sweet smell
The beautiful flower smell
Of thousands of others
Just like her
And life was good

She was just a little flower
Special/Different/Unique
And like every other flower
Beautifully naive
Completely unaware
Of the two-legged bea$t$
Who'd stop at nothing
To consume her sweetness
Di$turb & dominate her life of peace
Even if "their" greedy consumption
Brought about "their" own destruction

She was just a little flower
Who never bothered anyone
Till "they"" came...
To $teal her innocence
To control her mystery
& $ubjugate her soul
To eroticize & corporatize her beauty
Just to learn the $ecret of her bliss

She was just a little flower
She could have spared them "their" misery
Had "they" only come in peace

If "they" only had some manners
But since "they" didn't...
She didn't...
Before "they" even introduced themselves
"They" took what "they" wanted
And polluted her paradi$e

All "they" $aw...
Was a $weet little flower
And $he was $weet,
Real $weet!!!
$weet, $weet, Opium $weet
& so was her crazy cou$in Cocaine
"They" came, "they" $aw, and "they" took,
But got taken for a whole lot more
And the war was on

She was just a little flower
That still grows almost as beautiful
Somewhere on a once peaceful hillside
While "they"???
"They're" still crawling around...
Crawling ... whining ... begging ... crying...
Lost in "their" own madness
Still trying to find "themselves" in a world gone cold
Still looking for a way out of "their" self made hell,
Still searching for "their" souls.......

NOCHES SIN FIN CON ARTURITO

Noches encantadas con Arturito en nuestra Missión
Bailando a solas en mi sala
Viajando por los estados unidos de Radiolandia
Tiempos sagrados … una época inolvidable
El ambiente encendido con el sonido del mago musical
Un programa de Arturito en el radio era lo que me curó
Su voz hipnótica
Una estampa familiar llena de regalos antiguos
Regalos mas viejo que ninguna ciudad o campo o país
Nuestro sendero melodioso al cielo no tenía ni una frontera
La entrada melodica nunca estaba cerrada
Noches encantadas con Arturito
Su programa un lago sin fondo de orgullo y alegría
Querido Arturito, el mago musical de la Missión
Noches llena de la musica de su voz
Y la voz de su musica
Llena de la medicina que nos renació
Cada noche con Arturito
Una purificación después de dias de demasiado trabajar
Y un pasaporte ilimitado pá todo el pueblo mundial
Una puerta abierta pá America entera y
La sangre por dentro era el unico boleto
¡Ay bendito!
Noches preciosas, un remolino de recuerdos
Bailando frenéticamente
Embriagadas con el sabor de Arturito y su musica caliente
Siempre la gasolina de la máquina que era nosotros
Arturito y su programa picante era nuestra iglesia
Y su ritmo Caribeño iluminó el corazón del vencindario total
Pá mi,
Su musica, una cosa mas fuerte que calles desesperadas
Mas importante que estupideces superficiales
Una legada mas sólida que la turista oportunista y
Mas duro que los sueños ingenuos del pandillero
Asi, en estos dias,
Me encuentro bailando con recuerdos bellisimos
Noches calientes viviendo pá el sonido de su voz familiar
Noches encantadas con Arturito
Muchisimas gracias Compai por la luz eterna de su presencia
Querido Arturito,
Pá siempre jámas será el alma musical de la Missión

UNENDING NIGHTS WITH ARTURITO

Nights in the Mission District with Arturito were magical
Dancing all alone in my Living Room
Traveling through our united states of Radio-land
The times were sacred … An unforgettable era
Atmosphere on fire with the sound of our musical Magic Man
One of Arturito's radio programs was all it took to cure me
His hypnotic voice
A familiar comforting symbol full of ancient gifts
Gifts older than any place, city, or nation
Our melodic highway to heaven had no border
Harmonious, the entrance was never closed
Nights with Arturito were magical
His program a bottomless lake full of happiness & pride
Dear Arturito, musical Magic Man of the Mission
Nights were full of the Music of his voice
And the voice of his Music
Full of the kind of medicine that always brought us back to life
Every night with Arturito
Was an unlimited passport for the entire community
A healing ceremony after days of too much back-breaking work
And an open door to the Americas from North to South
The only Ticket you needed was the character of your essence
What a blessing!
Precious nights, a whirlpool of memories
Dancing wildly, a joyful frenzy
Drunk on the energy of Arturito & the heat of his Music
Always the necessary fuel for the machine that was us
Arturito & his spicy Radio Show was our church
His Caribbean Rhythms lit up the heart of our neighborhood
For me,
His music was stronger than the despair in the streets
More important than superficial stupidity
A legacy that will last longer than opportunistic tourists
And a whole lot tougher than the naïve dreams of Gang-Bangers
So these days,
I find myself dancing with beautiful memories
Hot nights living for the warm familiar sound of his voice
Magical nights with Arturito
Thanks Compai, for the never-ending light of your presence
My dear Arturito,
You will always & forever be the Musical Soul of the Mission

LA REGLA DE LOS LADRONES

La Frontera
Grandisima fantasía
Laberinto malvado
Una monstruosidad increíble
Una mentira mortal
Hecho de alucinaciónes santificadas
La Frontera
Una linea imaginaria
Nacido de la muerte y una dieta de misería
Esta pesadilla venenosa
Fortificada de un montón de codicia
Solamente una soga moderna de hipocracía ilimitada
Una ilusión cruel
La Frontera
Un cuchitril lleno de bobería desmoralizada
Una casa grande creada de robo
Y nadando
En bañeras calientes de lágrimas importadas
La Frontera
Una linea pá esconder un concepto artificial
Alrededor de vallas invisibles
Muros transparentes pá proteger tierras robadas
La Frontera
Dos palabras endiabladas
Dos palabras malvadas
Dos palabras sucias
Reglas de
Ladrones bestiales que no tienen derecho de existir
En la tristeza indescriptible del corazón
De esta vieja Poeta negra

THE DIVINE LAW OF THIEVES

The Border
A bigger than life fantasy
An evil maze
An incredible monstrosity
A deadly lie
A creation of sanctified hallucinations
The Border
An imaginary line
Born of death & fed on misery
This poisonous nightmare
Armed & held up by a mountain of greed
Just a modern day noose of unlimited hypocrisy
And cruel trickery
The Border
A hole full of Soul stealing stupidity
A mansion created by thievery
And swimming
In hot tubs of imported tears
The Border
Just a line hiding an artificial concept
Around invisible fences
Transparent walls to protect stolen lands
The Border
Two demonic words
Two evil words
Two filthy words
Laws of
Thieves & bullies that have no right to exist
In the too awful for words sadness in the heart
Of this old black Poet

NATURAL LOGIC

Even
The exhausted blade of grass
That breaks through the concrete
Listens
To the Wind's Song
And
Knows that it would be foolish
To do otherwise

INDESTRUCTIBLE
(HAITI MYSTIC GARDEN OF DREAMS)

Mama Haiti
Beautiful magical incubator
Mother of miraculous visions
You are the Sacred Womb of our freedom
Still infused with
The spiritual integrity of Boukman
You are the divine Light
The driving force
The seed that fed the dreams of
Anacaona & Toussaint Louverture
You are the intangible source
That ignites the fire inside
The underlying unifying sincerity of a
Jean Jacques Dessalines
The promise in your voice cuts through steel
A mystical Machete that sings through Rara prowess
And the whole world drinks your tears
Trying to wash themselves clean on your pain
Mama Haiti
The fiend of greed may have tried to kill your economy
And blindly deforest the wealth of your Souls
"They" may have desecrated your rice fields, but
You always bounce back
You are the Light
And right now you shine on the newest incarnation of
"The Emperor has no clothes"
Your unbreakable Spirit is so powerful
That even "his story" blushes
At the whispered
International embarrassment of having to admit defeat
Defeat at the hands of determined Black peasants
Defeat of the worlds' strongest Armies
Defeat … a bitter pill … an off-key soundtrack
Salt in the wounds to accompany the fall of an Empire
And still you're paying for it
Paying for an evil not of your making
Still paying in bloody deprivation for
That "behind whipping" that left Napoleon crawling
Beautiful Haiti
Sacred Womb of freedom
Hold on

The Emperor has no clothes
And you are the Light
The whole world finally sees
Sees right through the obscenity of his nudity
And it's not a pretty picture
Majestic Haiti
Proud incubator of independence
I, too, bathe in your sorrow, but
After so long eating from the bowl of poverty
There is no Hurricane, or Earthquake
Strong enough to re-enslave you
You may be stunned, knocked down for a minute, in shock
But "they" will never knock you out
Just like they couldn't lock you out of the Palace Gates
The proof's in the memory of the strength of your piss
A communal gift of poor Folks piss
Eating its way through the aluminum plated greed
Of sanctimonious despots
And we will not see you be defeated
Mama Haiti, you are our Ashé
Our never-ending unbeatable Spirit of freedom
You are the Light
Your Spirit is immortal
And this time
The best of humanity is ready to help you be reborn

ELS © '06

FREE LIKE THE BIRDS
or
THE REAL DEAL ON WHY YOU BETTER HIDE YOUR HEAD
IF YOU SEE A PIGEON FLYING BY

Henry Sylvester Lee the 3rd was sure one mean boy! He was always stealing & lying & picking on little tiny kids & real small girls....... especially Sara Mae Jones (who just happened to be the new kid on the block.) Sara Mae was quiet. She was one of those slow talking, shy Southern girls, and about as country as they come! Her Mama said, "Nice girls don't fight," and she always listened to her Mama!! Sara Mae Jones was Henry's meanest dream come true, he'd been waiting for her all his life!!!

She was a good girl! Tooooo good!! You know, the kind that was always polite ...one of those "yes Ma'am, no Sir" kinda girls. She took dance lessons & was always nice & never got into fights & always got good grades! All the teachers liked her, all the other kids liked her, even the Principal liked her!!! I mean, like everybody liked little Sara Mae ...everybody except for Henry Sylvester Lee the 3rd, who didn't like anybody......... (especially anybody that nice!) So Henry made it his mission in life to knock some of the niceness out of Sara Mae Jones!!!!!!!

Every day after school he would wait for her, 'cause Sara Mae was a guaranteed good time! He could trip her & punch her, and she wouldn't fight back. He could try to get her in trouble & embarrass her, and she wouldn't fight back. He could lie on her, pinch her, pull her hair, and she'd just stand there and cry! She'd never say a word, much less fight back. She couldn't!!! Her Mama said, "good girls don't fight," and she always listened to her Mama!

"It's a downright dirty shame!!!!!" folks would say. Everybody felt kinda sorry for little Sara Mae, but no one did a thing to make anything any different! So Henry just continued on his mission, and she quietly tried to stay out of his way. But, trying to stay away from Henry Sylvester Lee the 3rd was like trying not to get wet in a hurricane! It got so bad, she started cutting school to avoid him. And instead of playing Jump-rope & hanging out with the other girls, she started going to the park & feeding the pigeons. They were always happy to see her, and Henry didn't know where she was................. until he found her!

When Sara Mae started ditching school, Henry started hanging around outside her house. And when she came out, he'd follow her ...ducking behind cars & trees like a thief in the night. The park??? He couldn't believe it!!! There she was, "Little Miss Goody Two Shoes," hanging out in the park with the winos & bums, feeding the pigeons. Looked like she was having a great old time playing with the birds, running around & giggling and acting silly. It was weird, she'd chase those ugly, dirty Pigeons, and then they'd turn around & chase her. It even looked like she was having fun, and he couldn't stand that! "She wasn't supposed to have fun & be happy... She was supposed to be scared......., real scared......... Scared of him!"

He wasn't about to let his good thing go! So one day, when he couldn't take anymore, he ran over & knocked over her bag of breadcrumbs & kicked her in both shins!! She hollered & cried and he fell out laughing, ...'til the pigeons started using him for target practice. And for the first time in months, Sara Mae broke out in a big smile & started laughing real loud!!!! So loud, Henry could still hear her laughing a block away as he ran home.

"Laugh at him???"

"Laugh at him???"

"Laugh at him!?!?!?!"

Henry couldn't let a shy little country girl like that get away with laughing at him! So he'd plant himself outside her house like a tree, and wait & wait & wait 'til she'd try to sneak out. He followed her wherever she went, like an unwanted shadow, harassing her all the way. He was going to make sure she'd never forget laughing at Henry Sylvester Lee the 3rd. He stuck to that little girl like white on rice! "It's a pity, an outright sin, the way that low-down, rotten boy goes on bullying that nice little girl! Sara Mae just doesn't deserve to be treated like that," the neighbors would say (as they self-righteously did nothing to stop him!)

Sara Mae stopped studying ... she couldn't think! That mean, crazy Henry was everywhere! She couldn't sleep 'cause he marched through her dreams every night, and made her every day a nightmare. Her teachers & the Principal said they were worried about her as they watched her withdraw and watched her grades go down, but they wouldn't do anything to stop Henry. "After all, he's just a little boy," they said. "It's probably just a phase he's going through, and he'll outgrow it!"

By this time Henry's mission had turned into a crusade, and Sara Mae was spending more & more time with the pigeons in the park. All the other kids said, "Henry's a creep, a hope-to-die coward, and you just need to knock him down once. Sock him just once and he'll leave you alone!!!" But her Mama said, "Good girls don't fight," and she always listened to her Mama. So the kids just shook their heads and walked away. They figured, "She was kinda strange anyway, always hanging out in the park with those nasty pigeons. Mm, mm, Mmm, Mmm, Mmm! Anyone who'd rather be hanging out with those creepy birds in Wino Park had to be a little more than out to lunch!"

It wasn't long before she stopped going to her dance lessons, and quit going to school all together. She got quieter & quieter. She was never much of a big time talker, but she was never this quiet! The last person she really tried to talk to was her Mama. But when her Mother told her she ought to forgive Henry, "The boy probably just gotta a crush on you," she decided right then & there that talking to anyone was a waste of time. Nobody was going to listen to her, and nobody was going to stop Henry.

She knew everybody thought she was crazy, hanging out in the park with all the pigeons & all those old folks that nobody listened to anymore, just like nobody listened to her ... but she didn't care. The bums & winos never beat her up, and the pigeons would sing & talk & play with her all day. And she could say anything she wanted ..... they were always happy to listen. Even when she didn't have anything for them, they were still happy to see her. They'd crowd around her and follow her all over the park, and they loved it when she chased them & danced for them & threw breadcrumbs at them.

People said mean things about pigeons, just like they said mean things about her, but she knew better. They were her friends, and they weren't dirty & nasty like everybody said. She'd watch them clean their own feathers & clean each other. She watched them take care of each other, and she watched them fly way up in the sky & only come down when they felt like it. She liked the way they could fly high up above the crazy, mean people like Henry Sylvester Lee the 3rd. They were free as the wind and they knew it, and she was their friend & they knew that too!

For Sara Mae the park was a paradise. She never had to worry about having to hide from Henry in "Wino Park," because anytime he'd come anywhere near her those "filthy pigeons" would start up their target practice. Sometimes he thought he must be wearing a bulls-eye 'cause they never seemed to miss. And every time they got him, Sara Mae would fall out laughing & laughing & laughing. That park, that everyone made fun of, held the key to Sara Mae's freedom & Henry's hell!

She became an expert at hiding from Henry. Sometimes she'd get up real early in the morning, climb out the back window & down the fire escape, and she'd already be in the park before Henry woke up. There were times she'd see Henry trying to hide across the street, and she'd stand there in the middle of all those pigeons jumping up & down & laughing at him. He'd always look kinda confused, ...confused & angry. And every once in a while he even looked kinda scared, and that made her laugh even harder! "She musta been outta her mind! Nobody with any sense messed with Henry Sylvester Lee the 3rd!!" It was too much for him! He was furious, ...madder than mad!!! "That goofy little girl was gonna have to pay big for this one! Nobody got away with making fun of him!"

Henry wasn't used to being afraid of anybody, but Sara Mae

Jones & her nasty bomb squad had gotten on his last nerve. Henry was terrified & he knew it, and so did Sara Mae! He couldn't stand that! It was bad enough being scared, but knowing that she knew it & probably loved ever second of it was making him crazy. "It was time for that little hick to be taught a lesson she'd never forget!"

He had to find out how she was getting to the park without him seeing her. And when he did, he started getting up in the middle of the night so he could follow her & work on his plot. All he could think of was getting even ... his big payback! So he got a big bucket and started filling it up with the nastiest, gooiest, stinkiest mess he could find. When it was full, he climbed up on her roof as quietly as a snake in the grass & waited. "She had to be nuts, laughing at him!" He'd fix her & teach her once and for all that nobody messes with Henry Sylvester Lee the 3rd!!!

Sara Mae came sneaking out the window as the sun began sneaking up over the horizon. She was smooth as an alley cat as she came down the fire escape. She moved as softly as she could ... didn't want to wake up her Mama. And she was almost to the ground, when Henry emptied his bucket all over her. She could almost feel Henry's big grin, as the slime oozed down her face & inched it's sticky, smelly way down her little body. It was so slippery she lost her grip, and fell about two or three feet to the pavement. She couldn't keep the little yell from coming out & she couldn't stop slipping in the sloppy mess and falling back down every time she tried to stand up. She didn't want to wake anyone up, but the racket was waking everybody up & they were all coming outside & they were all looking straight at her & they were all laughing at her every time she fell back down in the nasty mess. She could hear Henry's Mom & Dad screaming about how mean & evil he was, but she could still hear Henry's loud laughing as the crowd got bigger & bigger & bigger.

She couldn't help shaking like a leaf, she was so mad! Someone helped her to stand up and get out of the puddle of slime, but it was still all over her & everyone kept on laughing! She couldn't stop the tears that made little lines like rivers down her face. And she couldn't stop the wanting to get even, even though she could still hear her Mama saying, "Nice girls don't fight!!" At that moment she wasn't feeling too nice, she just wanted to get away from there ... away from the slimy, stinky mess. Away from all the mean people! "AWAY!!! She just wanted to get to the park, and while some folks tried to hold her back she was still too slippery. She just pushed them away, and kept on walking & then she started running. The half-dressed crowd, still laughing, just followed. And she ran faster & faster & faster & faster!

Henry was feeling like Superman! He never laughed so hard in his life, that is until he got to the park and got a chance to see her face better. Something was different, her face had changed! Oh yeah, she still had tears running down her face & she was still shaking like a leaf, but she didn't look scared anymore. I tell you when she walked in that park, something spooky happened! It was like hundreds & hundreds & hundreds pigeons came from everywhere, and got all around her & snuggled up real close to her like they were trying to keep her warm. There were so many birds around her that you couldn't see her face anymore. I want to tell you it was weird! So weird that everybody stopped laughing & the only sound you could hear was the sound of those birds. And those birds, all those hundreds of pigeons were shaking like a leaf, just like Sara Mae.

Nobody could say a word. Folks were so scared you could taste fear in the air, and everyone knew it was time to leave. People started backing away, but no one would take their eyes off the park (not even mean old Henry.) Then, without a warning, the pigeons started shrieking & screaming & flying like an out-of-control bomb squad!

SPLAT!

WHAM!

PLOP!!!

SPLAAAAT!!!!!!

The crowd ran, and the pigeons moved onto the Elementary School's roof, the Jr. High's roof, the High School's roof, and even the University's roof! They took over the top of Henry's house, the Grocery Stores, the Post Office, the Soda Shops, and all the Movie theaters. It was almost like they were trying to spray paint the whole city!

Folks tried to keep it kinda quiet, but SPLAAAT!!! How do you stay quiet about an every day pigeon attack?? How do you not say anything, when nobody's seen little Sara Mae Jones since that day in the park??? How do you stay quiet and pretend that nothing really happened, when Henry Sylvester Lee the 3rd never leaves his house anymore unless he's going to school, or his parents make him go to the Post Office?

I know it's kinda hard for most people to believe, but I get reminded every time I see Sara Mae's Mama out there in the park feeding those pigeons. It's even harder to believe that.....

PLOP!!!

That pigeon that just got you didn't really mean it. We've seen the truth, and you & I know those pigeons aren't really interested in using us for target practice! That's just Sara Mae & her buddies looking for Henry!!!

I guess they always will,

......SPLAAAAAAAAT!!!

See what I mean?

UN SUEÑO DE BIEKE (5/26/2001)
(PA "TASO" CARLOS ZENON, NILDA MEDINA& JACKIE SANTOS)

¡Oye! ... ¡Oye!

¡¡¡BUUUN!!!

¡Las voladuras de bombas!

¡Bombas aterrorizandolos!

¡Bombas volando!

¡¡¡BUUUN!!!

Que sonido horripilante ... este gritón del diablo

¡¡¡BUUUN!!!

"Es un juego", dice La Marina ... Jugando amuchachados,
Jugando a ciegas con sus juegos de la muerte y la vida
Como mocosos mimados totalmente insensible al llanto mundial
Esta Marina y su banda de pandilleros internacionales
A sangre fria, despiada y llena de arrogancia ... ¿Jugando?
¡No! La Marina perdio el alma en la mugre de su barbarismo

¡¡¡BUUUN!!!

Y yo aqui, sentada cómoda en San Francisco
Escuchando atentamente a las palabras de Don Taso
Palabras bravas y poderosas, pero humildes
Palabras poeticas de un pescador, palabras de un sabio
Este Tipo es un rey, un sabio luchando pá La Isla Nena
Mas que otro pescador nadando en un mar de lágrimas
Nadando en lágrimas
Por falta del sabor de un pecadito en la cocina
Lágrimas por falta de ir de pesca pá la gente
Lágrimas porque no sirve ná esta rompecabeza de locura
Un juego hambriento que come la naturaleza y la paz
Mientras que el pueblo de la isla come casi ná

¡¡¡BUUUN!!!

Aqui en San Francisco
Mirando en los ojos de una profesora apasionada y dedicada
Y me encuentro cayendo adentro de un sueño de Bieke
Un sueño del amor profundo pá la gente invencible de Bieke
Un sueño noble ... un sueño sin cesar
De palmas regias y una belleza indescriptible
Y chamaquillos jugando y disfrutando todos los días sin miedo
Mirando hondamente en los ojos de la Doña Nilda
Y siento la gran tristeza de la gente de Bieke
Este pueblo, víctimas de una guerra no declarada y me duele

¡¡¡BUUUN!!!

Y lloro y escribe ... y lloro y escribe y lloro y lloro y lloro
La tinta de mi pluma esta hecha de mi llorar

Porque ayer tuve el mismo sueño de la misma arrogancia
El sueño del mismo machista militarismo
Con las mismas promesas de caramelos y riquezas
Promesas azucaradas pá embobar el mundo entero
¡¡¡BUUUN!!!
Regalos ensangretados pá los desafortunados ... víctimas como
Los de Somalia, de Tejas, Amazonas, de las Indigenas americanas
Los de Palestina, la gente Filipina, y el pueblo valiente de Bieke
La Marina, siempre jugando ... tirando mas y mas y
Mas víctimas disponibles en su montón de leña
Mas y mas víctimas de este juego estupido de guerra
¡¡¡BUUUN!!!
Y yo aqui en San Francisco
Musica, Poeta y Loca sin una peseta
Yo no tengo ná ... nada mas que mis sentimientos frustrados
Asi me siento aqui llorando como una cascáda de agua
Y escribo este poema de admiración con mis lágrimas
Escribo este poema con un corazón lleno de respeto
¡¡¡BUUUN!!!
Lo veo ... Toda via un extranjero en esta tierra extraña
Compai Jackie ... hijo verdadero de La Isla Nena
Caminando orgullosamente por las calles de esta grandisima cui-
dad
Un Campesino sin Campo, todavia perdido en el cemento
Pero todavia puro Jibaro y todo lo bueno que significa eso
Compai Jackie, ingenioso
Su presencia una sombra de tristeza, nostalgia y esperanza
Aun que vive el milagro de su sonrisa a pesar de todo lo que pasó
Y siempre una cara iluminada como el sol de un nuevo día
Así ... esta noche puedo dormir cómoda en San Francisco
Y voy a dormir en paz ... una paz anciosa
¡¡¡BUUUN!!!
¡Las voladuras de bombas!
¡Bombas aterrorizandolos!
¡Bombas volando!
¡Oye! ... ¡Oye!
¡¡¡BUUUN!!!
Me voy a dormir nadando en la fé inmovible de mis amigos
Porque el pueblo sabe que esta pesadilla increíble pasará
Y una gran libertad llegará pá la isla de Bieke
Eso lo siento hasta el hueso
¡¡¡BUUUN!!!
¿¿¿Se acabó??? ... ¡¡¡NO!!!
¡Pero viene!
¡Ya viene!

¡Viene como un aguaje! ... ¡Como ondas sin cesar!
¡Y nada, ni nadie puede para la libertad!
Bieke ... tu eres una estrella entre estrellas
Y todo el mundo te espera, preciosa Isla Nena
Y bailará el universo cuando llegue el día de tu libertad
Y las bombas serán nada mas que pesadillas
Memorías inolvidables de un tiempo pasado
¡¡¡BUUUN!!!

A DREAM OF VIEQUEZ
(FOR "TASO" CARLOS ZENON, NILDA MEDINA& JACKIE SANTOS)

Listen! ... Listen!

BOOOM!!!!!!

Blasts of Bombs!

Terrifying Bombs!

Bombs exploding!

BOOOM!!!!!!

The horrible blood curdling sound ... the devil's roaring scream

BOOOM!!!!!!

"It's just a game", says the Navy ... "The boys are just playing"
Blindly playing, like spoiled brats, with their toys of life & death
Everybody in the world is crying, but these boys could care less
The Navy & its bunch of international gangsters
Merciless, cold blooded & full of arrogance ... Playing??? No!
This Navy's lost its soul playing in the filth of its own brutality

BOOOM!!!!!!

And here I am, sitting comfortably in San Francisco
Listening hard to every single word of a guy named Taso
Strong & angry ... proud, but humble words
A wise man fighting for the people of La Isla Nena Viequez
This guy's a king
More than just another Fisherman swimming in a sea of tears
Swimming in tears because there are no fish in the kitchen
Tears because he can't go fishing
Tears because this puzzle of madness serves no purpose
It's just a hungry game that dines on Peace & eats Nature
While the people of the Island eat next to nothing

BOOOM!!!!!!

Here in San Francisco
Looking in the eyes of a serious & dedicated Teacher
And I find myself falling into the middle of her dream of Viequez
A dream of her profound love for the people of Viequez
          (a people who will never give up)
A noble & unending dream of majestic Palm Trees &
A natural beauty beyond description & children playing
And enjoying themselves every single day without any fear
I look hard & deep into the eyes of this woman Nilda
And I can feel the sadness of the people of Viequez
These beautiful people, victims of an undeclared war & it hurts

BOOOM!!!!!!

And I cry & I write ... & I cry & I write & I cry & I cry & I cry
I write ... with my pen full of ink made from all my crying

'Cause I had the same dream about the same arrogance yesterday
A dream about the same old Military madness
With same old promises of sweetness & prosperity
Sugar coated promises designed to stupefy the whole world
BOOOM!!!!!!
Bloody gifts for the unfortunate … victims like
The people of Somalia, Texas, the Amazon, Indigenous Americans,
The Palestinians, the Filipinos & the brave people of Viequez
The Navy, still just playing … throwing more & more & more
Disposable victims on their ever growing pile of firewood
More & more victims of this stupid War game
BOOOM!!!!!!
And here I am stuck in San Francisco
Musician, Poet, wild woman … don't even have a Quarter
Nothing … just a whole lot of frustrated feelings
So I sit here … crying … tears coming down like a waterfall
This Poem of praise is written with those tears
This Poem is written with a heart full of respect
BOOOM!!!!!!
I see him … still a stranger in a strange land
Jackie, my Brother, true son of the Island of Viequez
Walking proudly through the streets of this great big City
Straight up Country Boy … still lost in the concrete
Still just as "country" & all the good things that "country" means
Jackie, an ingenious Brother
His presence a shadow of sadness, homesickness & hope
Still the miracle of his smile alive in spite of the horror of it all
And his face always lit up like the Sun on a brand new day
So … tonight
Comfortably in San Francisco, I can sleep
And I sleep in peace … an uneasy peace
BOOOM!!!!!!

Blasts of Bombs!

Terrifying Bombs!

Bombs exploding!

Listen! … Listen!

BOOOM!!!!!!

I'm going to sleep swimming in the unmovable faith of my Friends
Because they know this incredible nightmare is gonna pass
They know a powerful freedom is coming to the Island of Viequez
And I can feel it all the way down to my bones

BOOOM!!!!!!

Is it over??? … NO!!!

But it's coming!

It's already coming!

It's coming like a tidal wave … it's coming in unstoppable waves
And nothing & nobody can stop this freedom from coming
Viequez … you are a star among stars
Precious Isla Nena … the whole world is waiting for you
And the universe will dance on the day freedom comes to stay
And the only Bombs will be nightmares, bad dreams
Unforgettable memories of a time somewhere in the past

BOOOM!!!!!!

IT WAS THE VUDU THAT WE DO
(DEDICATED TO ISE LYFE)

We were introduced to Vudu* on that night
That unforgettable night when the lights went out in Bluesville
Brother Ise turned up the heat on the conscious warmth of his love
This young Blood
Wrapped the positive Blackness of his joy around us
Brazenly covered us in his creative juices &
The lights came on in the church of our souls

Hearts full of Poetry flowed ... a circle of candles glowed &
Waitresses ... hard working ... kept on working
Waiting tables in the dark
As we filled ourselves with the miracle of each other
It was Poetry night & we were on fire
High as only creativity could take you

More than a hundred of us stayed sitting there
Overflowing with Word Power, full of all kinds of creative Juju
Sitting there in the dark,
'Til more & more candles came out & flickered
In an almost syncopated rhythm with our Poetry
If it wasn't for our Poems, you could've heard a pin drop

Respect was the only rule ... an unspoken rule
But somehow everyone knew just what to do
It was Vudu!!!
It was so still you could feel the righteous pull
Feel Damballah showering the crowd with the wisdom of our roots
Like a breeze you could feel the wild passion of Shango
As he proudly danced circles through the mood in the room

It was Vudu!!! ... It was magic!!!
And all those that couldn't handle it ... split!!!!!
They were not missed!
They left us
In what had become a sacred once-in-a-lifetime sanctuary
Bluesville became more than a proclamation of the dues we'd paid

The Ancestral vibes came down hard &
Rode us all the way to togetherness
Declared this darkened nightclub a sacred space &
Pure love opened it's arms &

The vibe in this club helped us call in the Spirits

It was the power of Juju running loose all over the place
Something beautiful happened,
On the night the lights went out in Bluesville
That night the darkness drowned all the unnecessary drama
Took all the spotlight off all the empty plastic in our lives &
We let go of all our phony fronts & held each other's backs

When those lights went out, we couldn't hide behind our masks
The Juju took off every piece of our jewelry
Undressed us in the darkness
Danced with us in our involuntary nakedness &
The serpentine wisdom in our rainbow of truth
Came out of hiding in the dark

It was the magic of Vudu!!!
Naturally electric, a secure womb & we couldn't move
More candles appeared,
As more of the uneasy dropped their fears, but
Most were so into
The beauty of the night that we forgot about the darkness
Most of us were even shocked at the disruption
When the lights came back on

Still everybody cheered, as the Spirits disappeared & we realized
We got what we asked for & lost the magic that we had
Those who hide in the ruthless glitter of the light
Invaded our sanctuary, turned our temple upside down
Foul mouth drunks stomped all over our togetherness
Disrespect & "talking trash" became the name of the game

It was all about flash & cash & nothing was the same
Several of us prayed ... really prayed
For those lights to go out again
Yes we prayed,
To bring back the Vudu, all the spiritual magic we knew

I know it's there,
          somewhere,
                    it's there,
                              waiting ... waiting
Waiting for us
To find our way back to that holy place where creativity is all

I wanna know,
Where were you when the darkness opened Damballah's door?
Could you feel the awesome power of the Vudu that we do???????
I need some more!!!
What did you do when the lights went out in Bluesville???
Where were you?
Were you there, or did you run away scared??
Did you even care???
Were you listening that night when the Juju* talked to you???
It was the Vudu that we do!

ELS©'10

FLUTE-A-HOLIC

(FOR RAHSAAN ROLAND KIRK, JAMES SPAULDING, ERIC DOLPHY, MARACA, PAUL HORN, ELISE WOODS, SHIGEO TACHIBANA, ADELE SEBASTIAN, YUSEF LATEEF, DAVE VALENTIN, JAMES NEWTON, JOHN CALLOWAY, MASARU KOGA, TIM BARSKY, ROGER GLENN, MIGUELITO MARTINEZ, KENNY STAHL, FRANCIS WONG, QUIQUE CRUZ & HAFEZ MODIRZADEH)

I confess
No way to escape it
I'm a Flute freak
Wooden Flutes, Metal Flutes,
I get high on the sound of
Any kind of Flute
When I'm "down" & the 9 to 5 boredom
Tries to eat up my Soul
I just seek a melodic heat wave
Flute Songs Rahsaan strong
&
Ancient Andean Flutes
In any City
Will open hidden mystic pathways
Through the uncivilized jungles of civilization
I got a Flute thing
I can't help it
I'm a Flute freak
Clay Flutes, Bamboo Flutes
For me
It's a bliss trip
A Cleansing
When life gets out of hand
&
I don't think I can take anymore
I bathe myself in the sound of Flutes
The timeless medicine of
Cascading waves of dancing Flutes
Tunes
That turn the most sleepless of nights
Into rejuvenating celebrations
And with the
Deep purifying caress of the Persian Ney
I can cast away the concrete madness
&
Find myself renewed & healing
Washed clean & ready for anything

And there's no way to escape it
I have to admit it
I'm completely sprung
Flute Songs rooted in the heart of my Soul
And I just can't hide it
I'm the real deal, a bonafide Flute freak
Got to tell the truth & confess
I'm hooked
A one hundred percent
Down to the bone
Flute-a-holic!!!

LIFE ON THE CORNER
(WHERE TIME STANDS STILL)

Every day Slick would spend hours in front of the mirror. I mean, like it takes forever to get it together in between "nods". But together was what was happening & "together" was what Slick was all about (if you listened to him tell it!) First he had to get his "Get Up" ...and then the mirror ritual began. After a while he'd take a short break for his "Stay Up!" Then more mirror magic, until he was so fine he wanted to jump up & kiss himself!!! Then he'd stroll on out to his favorite corner to hang out with the "Fellas" & share himself (his great work of art) with the world. He was too cool for words (at least he thought so!)

But the real deal was..... Slick looked like he'd just slid all the way through hell & back again. Still, he knew he had it together. You could tell he just knew he had it all together by the sure-of-himself way he stood there. Posing for the Ladies. Mister too cool to sweat, dripping with pure arrogance. Raggedy hat all cocked to the side, holding on to his crotch like it was some kind of diamond mine. Leaning meanly ... Pimpwise! Sagging pants that had once been so tight you could damn near count his pubic hairs! But he was cool! Together?? Boy knew he looked good!

Slick would slide his eyes all over every female that walked his way! Never noticing how fast they walked by, trying to escape his glassy red eyes. Trying to escape the X-rated gaze that would climb their legs & crawl all up into their underwear as they raced by! But life was good in the "Hood," and Slick was patient! The boy was too cool to worry about their lack of taste. Knew he just had to stay there leaning on dreams & air. Hanging with the Homeboys 'til some Sweet Tender, a wonder woman worthy of his attentions, would float on by & choose him.

And then "She" appeared!!!!! A chocolate covered wet dream on legs! Their eyes locked & Slick knew it was on! They walked & talked for a long time, or maybe it was a short time. They walked & talked for what seemed to be the beginning of forever. They talked about big things, little things, everything. About the weird drama of life in the city, their likes & dislikes. They even talked about sappy movies & their off-the-hook families. Hey! "She" was even smart, not just another quick stepping sidewalk airhead! This one was a Keeper ... different ... the kind he might want to get to know better. The kind he might want to romance & impress... not just seduce & turn loose!

Then right as he was trying to make that smooth move & sneak up on a kiss, his nose started running like a faucet & just that quick he was sick as a dog. Dope sick!!! Nose running, stomach flipping, skin crawling. Broke out in a cold sweat! Jones coming down big time! Oh my God!!! Why now? Couldn't it have at least waited until after he had a chance to get down & "hit it." He just wanted a minute, or two, to get it on. Damn! Was that too much to ask? To "do the do," be normal & straight-up sweet & nasty with a Sistah. Oh well. He knew the ritual & there was no turning back. His real Lady was calling him & what could he do???

Girlfriend looked confused. He had seen that look before. Too many times before. And it was that time again. He was gonna have to choose. His real Lady was calling him & She never took no for an answer. So he looked deep in the "let's get it on" desire in Baby's eyes, borrowed $20 & left Girlfriend standing there. Said he'd be right back, but you know the real deal. Slick melted into Urban folklore, chasing intoxicating dreams. Dancing with death, while gambling with life on his same old scandalous "mission" as he slid deeper into the shadows. Went straight to the friendly neighborhood "Shooting Gallery" & "got right" & headed back to his same old Corner.

And there he remains, day after day ... year after year. Waiting for God knows what. Funky as hell, but still posing suggestively for the Ladies. Mister too cool to sweat, dripping with pure arrogance. Same old raggedy hat, still talking "smack" with the Fellas. Still holding on to his abstinent crotch like it was some kind of diamond mine. Leaning ... Pimpwise! Wearing the same old foul worn to shreds sagging pants that had once been so tight you could damn near count every single one of his pubic hairs! Knew it was his curse & his destiny to stay there leaning on air. Hanging with the Homeboys 'til some Sweet Thing, a hard working Molasses Mama worthy of his attentions would come strolling by & choose him. Still telling himself the same old over-worked lies.

"Nodding out" on his Corner, with his Homeboys, he was more than just another somebody stuck somewhere in the middle of nowhere. In this world he was a whole lot more than just another lost Junkie, trying to hide on a Corner where ain't nothing changing but the hands on the clock.

Life was good in The Hood & it was all just a matter of time!

SOLO UN ACTO DE CARIDAD

Cuando canta la Luna
Llora el Sol
¡Enfurecido!
Su gran egoísmo perdido entre dos luces
Pobrecito pucheron aparatoso
Echando bocanadas de envidia
Intimidado sin cesar por celos
Pero embrujado por su belleza silenciosa
Y encantado por el milagro de su regalo maravilloso
Y se dice el Viento
¡Que bueno esta nuestra naturaleza pasmosa!
Un ciclo humilde y sencillo
¡Ay bendito! … ¡Mira!
Que rica es
Dicen las estrellas
No hay una noche tan perfecta como esta
¡Coño! … Que tristesa
Dice el amanecer
Lo que tenemos es un mundo limpio, llena de belleza
Y todavia
Anegando en su propia arrogancia
La raza humana
Una raza confundida y sin corazón y
Engordándose de comer su gran falta de gratitud y
Disfrutándolo sin pensar
Ni una gota pequeñita de ternura en las venas
Pura sangre congelada
No puede ver
No quiere ver
Sentados cómodamente y ciegos en sus propios mundocitos
Sangrando condescendencia
Y se dicen
Ríendo en nuestras barbas
¿La Naturaleza? … ¡No Me digas!
Nada más que otra pérdida de tiempo precioso
¿A quien le importa esa bla bla bla?
Tirando más y más y más bochinche y hablando de ná
Solo un otro ciclo tan simple
¿¡¿Y que vale este?!?
Si existe
Solamente porque le mantengo la conexión

JUST AN ACT OF CHARITY

When the Moon sings
The Sun cries
Burning red hot with rage
Its overwhelming egotism lost in the Twilight
Pompous & pouting & looking pitiful
Puffed out of shape with envy
Completely intimidated by jealousy
But enchanted by her silent beauty
And charmed by the extraordinary miracle of her gift
And the Wind says
Mother Nature is astonishing
A humble, unassuming cycle
Aaaah … look!
It's exquisite
The Stars say
There is no Night as perfect as this one
Dammit, how sad!
Says the Dawn
We have a World that's full of pure beauty
And still
The Human Race
A race drowning in its own arrogance
Confused & heartless & making themselves fat
Eating too much of their own lack of gratitude &
Enjoying the whole thing without even a thought
Not one drop of tenderness in their veins
Blood frozen cold
Can't see
Doesn't want to see
Sitting comfortably blind in their own little worlds
Bleeding condescension & laughing in our faces
Saying,
Mother Nature?!? … You gotta be kidding!
Who cares about all this bla bla bla?
Just another waste of time
Throwing around more & more & more gossip
And talking about nothing
It's just another simple cycle &
How much can this one thing really be worth?!?
If it only exists
Because I don't pull the plug?!?

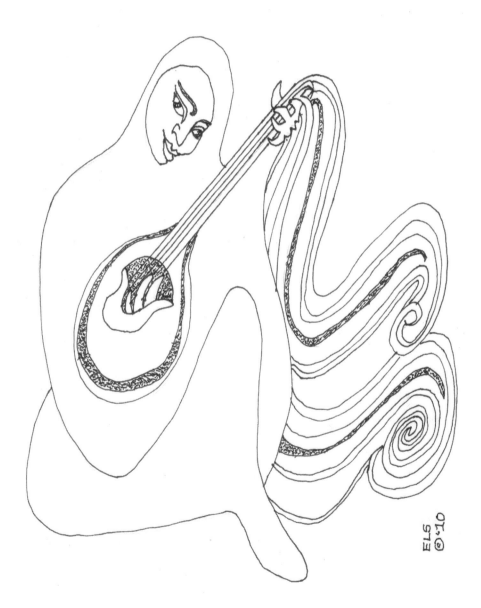

ELS
© '10

OCEANS OF SAND

(INSPIRED BY & DEDICATED TO SIMON SHAHEEN, OUM KHALSOUM, ROBERT MIRABAL, ELMAZ ABINADER, HAMZA EL DIN, NAWAL, BILL LOWE, RENDA DABIT, RAJAMANI, YAIR DALAL, JEWEL PARKER-RHODES, RUMI, RABIH ABOU-KHALIL, VALENTINA TIJERINA, AHMED ABDUL MALIK, MELANIE DEMORE, HAFEZ & YEGANEH MODIRZADEH, WARIS DIRIE, GIBRAN, DR. KARLTON HESTER, NUSRAT FATEH ALI KHAN)

There was no life in the land of the sand until you walked in
No! … You did not walk in!! … You arrived!!!
Your presence … elegant … air of royalty
A radiant bronze masterpiece
You were the unsung melody … moved like a Poem
You are a magnificent work of Art
A whole new kind of graceful
Tornado strong … yet humble
Smelling sweet
Like Frankincense wrapped in Henna painted power
A power way beyond new age constraints, or
The limits of time

Thousands & thousands & thousands of years in your walk
The theater of your eyes … black & wild
And peaceful & diverse as nomadic Tuareg
Or Tibet or Somalia or Marakesh
Indescribably awe-inspiring nights
In the ancient Kingdom of Kush
Kush, whose massive Army was always watched over by
The light of millions of seemingly tireless guardian stars
Always on guard

I could see the majesty of the desert in your eyes
A living, never-sleeping desert alive in your eyes
An ocean of sand, that doesn't know how to be still
A Pueblo Indian, Persian, Mongolian, African,
Falasha, Bedouin, Mexican, Lebanese,
Romany of the Kalahari, Rajisthani, Palestinian,
Feasting on figs from The Tree Of Life in The Garden of Eden
Unending crowds of
International miracle seekers in search of salvation
Still trying to find some begged-out Genie
Hiding inside Aladdin's lamp
Refusing to see the oceans of sand are wise
And the Genie has retired & his friends are all on strike
And there is no free Magic Carpet ride
The desert is a Mama & she never sleeps

It's in your eyes!
Land of sand … Womb of Prophets
Gnawa trance, Roma dance, a purification
A Navajo fire, Tuva chants, the excitement of Pow Wows
Nopales con huevos & Fry Bread
Your eyes
Bottomless, endless, black pools
Full of sacred pride & ecstatic joy
A gentle calm … a fierce beauty … a smoldering sadness
Very different, but
Strangely familiar rhythms Modern ancient songs
Mystic Dalit visions
Cosmic, fragrant, patterns

It's alive! … Feel the life!
Why do so many fools refuse to see the life???
The romance behind screens of Olive trees
And all the forbidden glances, hidden from
The watchful eyes of overprotective Parents
With other plans
For the hands of their disinterested Daughters
It's alive
In blooming Mesquite trees
The unmistakable aroma of Sage Brush
Sly Coyotes & the terrifying beautiful precision
In a Ballet of Dust Devils, little Twisters,
Spinning, whirling, inside the many sides of your being

You make me feel the desert
Pull me inside the logic & confusion
Of the Sandstorm in your eyes
Land of sand … Land of extremes
Land of starving Families & wealthy Sheiks
Of exquisite feasts of Cous Cous
Dates, goat's meat & Mint Tea
Sad eyed displaced Kangaroos with stomachs full of dreams
Land of Veils, Burkas & Bandit Queens
Hereditary Harems & Belly Dancing
Shrewd aggressive Market women,

The Undisputed Divas of "wheel & deal"
And happily silent submissive Matriarchs
Covered from head to feet

Land of sand … Land of extremes
Generations of Warlords sworn to the sword

Living right down the road from generations
Of folks who can't even conceive of
Hurting the deadly Scorpion or swatting a flea
Quiet, extremely pious, gigantic walled cities
And festive Berber Camps
Secure on strong backs of
Camels & Elephants strolling thru windstorms
Secret whispers ... stolen kisses from
Runaway Princes who reject tradition
And slip into the night with their Lovers & Mistresses
Like cactus flowers that run from the sun

And stories that ride on the wind
About Women
Who would rather be turned into pillars of stone
Than spend the rest of their lives as unhappy wives
And nights full of Fancy Dancing & Mystical Madayin songs,
Soothing drones, sacred, ageless sounds
Music of an Oud, the Tar, the Gimbri, or a Flute
Mesmerized by Balafons, Afro-Indian Jazz
And the rebellious fury of Rai
You opened my eyes
Jumped all in my face ... made me see
The desert is a Mama & she never sleeps

And then the Music stopped & you were gone
Even the whirling Sand Dervishes stopped dancing
Laughing ... at the pitiful arrogance
Of all the no listening listeners limitations
Magical, musical incantations
Laughing in the ignorant shadows
Of some imaginary
"Free market" Junk Food selling Oasis
Laughing at all the greed & conceit & over-inflated fantasies
Of long since deflated imaginations

And you split!
Straight up disappeared ... gone
Left us empty ... wanting ... wanting more
As the scent of
Night blooming Jasmine flowers & Black Orchids
Followed your unspoken promises
Right out the door
Nothing left of you ... not even a dream
Just a little tiny pile of sand in the middle of the floor

And an amazing Snap Shot inscribed in my mind
Of waving sands
The ages of Sages alive in your hands
The vast, proud, ever-changing beauty
Of this living land
Majestic land … your never sleeping desert

Mother of Scheherazade's brilliant wit
And the Poetic peace of Gibran
I can see it in the essence & elegance of you
The desert of you … that always comes alive
Every time
I think about the blackness of your eyes

QUEEN NINA
(OUR LIGHT IN THE TUNNEL)

Nina Simone was an eruption
Our artistic explosion of Black pride & power
In a nation tranquilized
By the blindness of its own arrogance
The presence of all she stood for
Reminded us of all our Ancestors lived & died for
Her Songs told the world
That we were worth more than just singing about
Sista was a live volcano
Uncontrollable … ready to erupt at any moment
She was the long-awaited reincarnation
Of Nzinga, Fanny Lou Hamer, Anacaona & Granny Nanny
A straight up in your face Sage, a Warrior
A woman brave enough to declare herself King
Nina Simone was an unveiled threat
An unheard of shocking out-in-the-open threat
A terrifying reality check
A made in America, too black to ignore omen
Chewing up stereotypes for breakfast, lunch & dinner
And for dessert
Kicking "the Man's" "lesser than" theories off their throne
Sista Nina's blacker than black magic was so powerful
She toppled "our" color caste system without even trying
The medicine of her voice kissed away the pain in us
Tore down the insurmountable walls of self-hatred in us
And gently wrapped us
Lovingly in a blanket of pride sweeter than Sugar Cane
Our Nina didn't ask to be respected
She commanded respect from the most disrespectful
And refused to accept anything less
In a nation stunned by
The absolute brilliance of her unquestionable talents
Nina Simone was the incarnation of the best in us
Our strengths, our weaknesses, our joys
She modeled the indisputable pain in us
The beautifully fierce, sensually proud, but
Frustrated Black genius of us
Her voice was
Our musical ticket to everywhere we've ever been
Her regal wizardry on the Piano keys was
A Time Machine & we were transported
From the Park bench to penthouses on Park Avenue

From the African savannahs to cane & cotton fields
From the humiliation of the segregated South
To big City slums & all the way into Carnegie Hall
The Spirit of always spoke to us through her
And I'm so grateful I had sense enough to listen

LA SAYA NEGRA

It was Silver Madness,
The fever of greed & las Minas de Potosí
An unholy alliance … an evil gluttony
That gave birth to
The massive importation of enslaved Africans
¡Que cosa endiablada!
These Africans,
As well as enslaved Indians,
Were forced to work & work & work & work & work
Work endlessly under conditions so barbarous
That they were guaranteed
A life expectancy of no more than 6 months
Despite these horrendous odds many survived
After emancipation Afro-Bolivians relocated
Went up into the Mountainous region of the Yungas
Only to find themselves trapped
Viviendo encarcelados en la belleza de Las Yungas
Tricked!!!
They'd been driven into another form of servitude
And removed so far from everything & everybody
That there was no way out
It took almost another 100 years of backbreaking labor
Before any semblance of emancipation would find them
And they would find a real reason to celebrate
These days,
An estimated 25,000 Afro-Bolivians live in Las Yungas
A resilient people, who still hold on to their traditions
They are a proud people who've fought non-stop to survive
There are many other settlements in Las Yungas, but
In the town of Mururata
They've kept the integrity of their culture so intact
That they even have the direct descendant
Of an African King still living there
In Bolivian culture the most obvious African influence is
Saya music, or simplemente La Saya
In Coroico a Carnival is celebrated every February
A tropical bacchanal in the equatorial Andes
With full Comparsas of Drummers, Singers, Dancers
And percussive instruments like the Bolivian Reco-Reco
(which is probably the world's longest Guiro)
Y me encuentro encantada
Standing, waiting,

Thirsty for the taste of our People's endurance
¡Yo! Una huérfanita perdida entre lobos que comen cultura
¡Yo! Familiar de sangre
¡Yo!
Standing, just another face, alone in a crowd of lost Souls
Lost Souls, frightening in their emptiness, shallow Souls
Blasé entertainment freaks
Culture vultures who have no idea of La Saya's significance
A Mob so lost in the Rhythm that they can't see the pain
They can't feel the pride & could care less that I cry inside
So with my heart still bleeding for & dancing with
The thousands of ghosts in & around the Mines of Potosí
Me encuentro encantada & I listen
I listen to the declaration of the Bells
The rattles of the dancers, the singing of Las Payas
The irresistible call of the Guiros & the powerful Bombo
The Afro-Bolivians are coming, dancing through my tears
Cantando La Saya a pesar de los malintencionados
La Saya a euphoric healing exorcism
La Saya, a mesmerizing rite, una semilla eterna de renacer
This musical ritual born of years of tears
Is a bath more purifying than the holiest of holy waters
Un grito Africano que nunca morirá
The Afro-Bolivians are coming dancing La Saya
Through my tears they come dancing
As the pain of rage tries unsucessfully to cover my ears
And in a louder than loud wild frenzy
The irreverant ecstatic crowd roars
LA SAYA NEGRA!!!

IT AIN'T EASY
(INSPIRED BY PURPLE MOON DANCE THEATER & DEDICATED TO ARISIKA RAZAK)

Being a Black Mama ain't easy
Even if you're straight as an arrow
First you've got to lie to your Kids
Cause you know, even if they're
The smartest Kids in the whole wide world
They can never be President here in
"The land of the free"
& no matter how much love you show them
They're being force fed all the myths
All the time
About their thick lips,
Loud mouths, big behinds & bad attitudes
Myths about
Being "rowdy, low-life, ignorant people"
And they're either too dark or too light
Got "ugly noses" & "bad hair"
That only looks "good"
When nobody can see it
And still you teach them
They're perfect just like they are
They're beautiful & smart &
Special & sweet
Just because they're yours
And then you've got to teach them to lie
To protect themselves
Against all that racism & sexism &
Racism & sexism & racism & sexism &
Racism & more racism & racism
Until hell freezes over &
The devil buys ice skates
And if you're a Lesbian
You've also
Got to teach your Children to lie
To protect themselves against
What society perceives as the
Negative legacy of having a "queer" Mama
Whose only crime is
Having the courage not to hide & to Proudly
Live with the Woman she loves
And on top of all that

After you've taught your Children to lie
To almost everybody
About almost everything
You've got to teach them
Never, never, never, ever to lie to you!!!!!!!
It's not easy being a Black Mama,
But the Ancestors were calling
Screaming for a new day
Another chance, a different way
And I really wanted to have a Baby
Or two, or three
I wanted to answer that call
To quiet that need
A call older & more important than me
A nagging that wouldn't stop & didn't stop
'Til that day I felt
That little Spirit moving inside my soul
That miniature miracle
Wildly dancing in my womb
Melting down all the ice
Life had wrapped around my heart
It's not easy being a Black Mama
Especially
If you just happened to "come out"
In the not so "good old days"
Days when Lesbian Mamas lived in terror
A never ending fear, that one day
Someone … anyone … a neighbor,
Your Church, a nameless enemy, a friend
Or some angry guy,
From some long ago forgotten time
A terrified, hurt & angry man
A man scared & blind with hatred, 'cause
Some fine Sistah was getting everything
He never even had a chance to get next to!
Hey! … Maybe even your own Mother
Would call the Authorities
And they'd come unannounced
They'd come … sneaking around
Like thieves to steal your Babies
To take your beautiful Children away
Not because you were an unfit Mother
Who misused, neglected, or
Brutalized her Children
NO!!!!!!!!!!!!!!

They'd take your Children
Because you were in love!
Because,
You'd found the Woman of your dreams
Because you'd finally found someone
Who made you love everything & everybody
Including your own Children more
Because you were happy, healthy &
Madly in love!!!
And that happiness was criminal
Was against the law
Was a mental disorder
An unspeakable perversion
So you lived in an ever-present fear
A fear that haunted your every day
And turned dreams into nightmares
And time stood still
'Til those Kids turned eighteen
And you could finally breathe again
It's not easy being a Black Mama...
Even if you're straight as an arrow
And if you're a single Black Mama
You become
An actress, a master juggler, a magician
A miracle worker who learns to turn
Peanut Butter & Jelly
Into major occasions for celebration
You learn how to dance
And duck & swerve like a Boxer &
Turn every stone thrown at you & yours
Into weight lifting exercises
That only make you stronger
But if you're a single Black Lesbian Mama...
Trying to make sense out of life after love dies
It's over   ... she's gone
And you???
You learn to deal with alone, but then
She comes around
Saying she can't see herself
Coming to hang out with the Kids
(That she helped raise)
If she can't see herself being with you!
And you wonder ... is Sisterhood
Only as real as the bed we share???
No help there!!!!!

Sounds like the re-run of a bad 3D movie
With a name like
"The Days When Turkey Basters Walked On Legs"
Those days of the not-so-ideal marriage
To the not-so-ideal ex-Husband
The "closet queer"
Who just sort of disappeared
When he realized
You'd no longer be his "front"
And you realized
An uneasy freedom
Is always more desirable,
Than the heavy chains
Of an unacceptable acceptability
But that still doesn't make it any easier
To be a Black Mama
It's like a lifetime working Double-time
And they don't give you Overtime
For putting food in your Children's mouths
While,
Pulling all those arrows out your back
From all the scared Sisters
Who forgot … you were their Sister!
From the thousands of Brothers
Whose dirty diapers you changed
Only to watch them grow & forget
That you're their Mother, and
All those "good friends"
Who claim to love you
As long as they never have to see you
With your Lover
And all those other Folks who refuse
To accept that your happiness
Is not dependent on their acceptance
No, it ain't easy being a Black Mama
But as long as clouds & Babies cry
And Stars dance in the darkest nights
Just one of those sweet "come to me" smiles…
On a proud Woman's face
Will always lift me when I fall
Keep my grateful Spirit flying high, and
Keep me strong enough
When times get rough
To keep on fighting on
Just one smile from a Child

Is like a "don't wanna give up" injection
Always pushes me
In that "we're gonna win" direction
And keeps me standing tall, reminding me
"Love is the only thing worth fighting for"
And that, I'll have to keep on fighting non-stop
For our right to love & be loved
Until this story no longer needs to be told
And nobody ever said it would be easy!!!

LISTEN TO THE RAIN
(PÀ LA VOZ INVENCIBLE DEL JIBARO ANDRES JIMENEZ)

El Yunque _____ Jardin de esperanza
Donde vive el alma Boricua
El alma de La Perla del Caribe

El Señor Gringo, he always listens
But never hears the Music
Of El Yunque
Too busy!!!
Always rushing, running
Taking, breaking, always taking
But never taking time enough
To listen to the Rain
To hear her sacred song
To feel the magic
The magic

Aiiiii _____ El Yunque
Gritando sangre de las flores
El llanto del Coqui

      "They" came
Suffering acute Gringo-itis
Of the bank account
"They" will never know
El Yunque is
      More
Than just another Rain Forest
      More
Than a beautiful Tourist Trap
      More
Than just one more "romantic locale"
With more great potential
For the "cultural expansion"
Of MacDonald's bullet proof hamburgers
      BORICUA
Have you ever listened to the Rain
The magic

El Yunque sagrado
Oración de la Lluvia
Corazon de la Tierra
Pesadilla de Los Yanquis

Listen Boricua
Listen to the rain
El Yunque
Is a fertility dance
It's Borinquen's Poem of power
Don Pedro, Doña Lolita, Don Juan Antonio
Tried to make you hear
Tried to make you feel strong enough
To live for a Tree
And maybe die to be free
Did you hear them
The magic

Aiiiii _____ El Yunque
Sombra de anhelos escondidos
El renacimiento del sueño Borincano

Listen Boricua
Listen to the Rain
Let her whisper in your ears
Let her shower you with pride
Let her overwhelm you with her beauty
Let her lead you to the magic
El Yunque
Is Nature's declaration of independence?
Let the rhythm of the Rain
Burn like fire in your blood
Have you ever really listened to the Rain???
Listen Boricua!
Listen!!
Listen to the Rain!!!!!
Boricua _____ listen!
Listen!

ROBLESQUE
(TO AL ROBLES WITH LOVE)

¡Silencio! Al Robles is missing
It's way too quiet around here these days & we miss him
This one of a kind poetic daredevil
Transplanted culture personified … Adobo con Bebop
With an awe-inspiring playful impish smile
That always let the best in us know we were at home
Lifting up tradition anytime it lost its balance & tried to fall
Trading the tallest of tales in the park
Conjuring strength in ageless Spirits older than time
Or locked in a musical trance, happy to be completely
Under the spell of a Bobby Enriquez tune @ Bajones
A Pinoy Homeboy on a mission
The strength of his soul reborn with every Poem
A loveable rascal defying description
¡Silencio! Where is he?
Al, the Fillmore Flipster
Stalking creativity with a vengeance
Finding pieces of creativity & truth everywhere
In everything
The eternal essence of intelligent existence
Leading him on, dancing word circles all around him
There were days when none of it made any sense, but
Then it was funny & beautiful, ridiculous or ugly
More than once it was both inspiring & tragic
Historic landmarks in the making, a blossoming
Myth building Poems, tons of Stories needing to be told
And they came pouring down like an unstoppable flood
A furious Waterfall
Out of the mouths of angry misused Farm Workers, and
Found themselves all tangled up in the irony of
A meal of Pilipino Soul Food
With a side of Mangos & Collard greens for dessert
¡Silencio! If you were you listening
You could see the tongue-in-cheek brilliance in the way
He tasted every word as they rolled out of his mouth
In the way he digested the ambiance of Poems being born
And followed the rhythm of words as they came swaggering
Dancing in the streets of North Beach & Cesar's Latin Palace
Squashed inhibition & found a good part of his heart in the trance
Of hotter than hot Jam sessions @ Jimbo's Bop City
Al, a Fillmore Flipster, a clever predictable trickster

The undisputed Poet Laureate of Manila Town
Who comfortably wrapped himself in a mixture of
Smiley Winters, Kulingtang, Flip Nuñez & Sarah Vaughan
   ¿Silencio? The Muse is in mourning
But there will never be enough tears
To wash away the legacy of his vision
The spiritual pride & integrity of his Poetry
Lives in the resurrection of the I-Hotel
Hides behind the hungry laughter of city slick Hustlers
Is buried beneath stolen visions & the exposure of
Soulless, big-time, urban magicians who sell fantasies
To the disillusioned
His powerful word magic conjured
The reclamation of otherwise unacknowledged young men
Young men who'd left their all a world away
On the other side of a sea of broken dreams
But never forgot to take the time to heal, rejoice & laugh
As they partied, gambled, danced the Cha Cha & romanced
Nights & sore backs away @ the California Hotel
Held up the economy on Columbus & the clubs on Broadway
And almost wore out the pavement up & down Kearny & Grant
Then came to on the same old farms picking fruit the next day
   ¿Silencio?
NO! There is no sadness strong enough
To erase the hipness of his vision
Al Robles, our Fillmore Flipster, our eternal trickster
Magnificent Manong!
It will never be over & we will not be silent!!!

175

MY COUNTRY 'TIS OF THEE

Damn thing always starts the same way! Always the same way. No new thing. Nothing original. Same damn thing & I can always feel it coming on before it happens. I just can't stop it!! Any loud noise is the enemy. I try to stay away from loud noise … any noise … all noise. It never works. Sometimes it looks like noise just likes to follow me around. And when it finds me it's just the same old thing. Same ole same ole, like a re-run movie. Like a re-run nightmare!! There's nowhere to hide & no way to stop it. First the big BANG! Then the buzzing inside my head … ringing in my ears. Next the dizziness & then "THEY" start coming!!!

RUNNING … YELLING … AN ALL CONSUMING CHAOS
OUR SIDE … THEIR SIDE … ANY & EVERYBODY'S SIDE
BLOOD THIRSTY DEMONS
MANIC & VIOLENT & OUT OF CONTROL
WIRED!!!
LIKE A HUNGRY AVALANCHE ON SPEED
SHOUTING ALL OVER
SCREAMING ALL AROUND ME
"THEY'RE" COMING
COMING FROM EVERYWHERE, COMING AT ME
STRAIGHT FOR ME!!!!!
"THEY'RE" GONNA GET ME, MURDER ME
THE COUNTRY, MY FAMILY, TORTURE ME, TURN ME INTO HAMBURGER!!!
AAAAAAAAH!!!!!

"Always keep a cool head!" "BE ALL YOU CAN BE!" "Be a MAN, a real MAN!" That was "THE WORD/THE LAW," but it never worked! It still doesn't work. "THEY" just keep on coming & it's pure undiluted fear, blind crazy fear, violent uncontrollable fear! The kind of fear that makes you afraid of yourself. A man?!? What the hell are "THEY" talking about? I am a MAN! A real man! A one-hundred-percent man! But when "THEY" start coming at me I'm scared shit-less. Scared out of control. People tell me I fight City Buses. Say I scream, curse, act real ugly, attack moving trucks. I know it's true, it's got to be. Friends & Family have seen me go off. Held me down so I won't hurt myself. So I won't hurt anybody else. I've been arrested & hospitalized for it, so it's got to be true. They always release me. I'm harmless, the authorities say. "Just a little shell-shock."

Shell-shock??? That's what they always say about you, when something you don't remember makes you do things that you don't understand & don't know anything about until someone else tells you about them. SHELL-SHOCK!?! Shit! "Boy's war crazy, but harmless"

Yeah, harmless! That's so sad it's funny, but I'm not laugh-ing!! Even when I was a kid, I was always considered harmless. I

176

was never a fighter. Guys on the "Block" called me a lame-ass bookworm, too soft, too gentle. Too gentle that is … 'til I got to "Nam." The Authorities still have the nerve to say "harmless." Only now I scare people … scare myself. Folks think I'm crazy, violent, nuts! Folks say that when I got to "Nam" I went out of control & never came back. They say I got lost in the madness & never found my way home. God, I wish I never saw a uniform, a gun, the Military, the blood. Vietnam was a blanket of blood, a murderous orgy married to blizzards of blood!

A battlefield, anywhere, is always the grimmest tale in a self-righteous theater of the macabre. An uncontainable fury, an acceptable lunacy, a deluge of blood, blood & more blood! It's a pure, unadulterated, one-hundred-percent, death-dealing bloodbath running around in the nude. OH GOD!!! It's like being locked in a ballet of bloodshed! A bizarre ghoulish contest between finely-tuned killing machines. INESCAPABLE MURDER ! … EVERYWHERE MURDER & MORE MURDER!!!!!!

And I murdered! I had to murder, or be murdered. And when sanity surrendered to the madness of reality my soul just got up & ran off. I felt it leave. I felt the light go out in the space that once held my heart & saw what was left of my soul disappear. I know some little remnant of the man that was me is still roaming around out there trying to find a way home. Looking for a way to escape "the War" … trying to get away from any & all wars!

And I cried. Like an out-of-control banshee, I fell down on my knees & I cried. Crying & praying that the last tear was the last tear. As I watched it falling deep down inside the shadowy jungle of lost minds & all the nameless souls that were left behind.

And … Oh God … I … I … I wish & I wish & I wish & I…….

EL LLANTO DEL BERIMBAU
(INSPIRED BY MESTRE CARLOS GILBERTO ACEITUNO)

Iyé viva meu Mes camara
I heard you
El llanto del Berimbau
The Theme Song on the road to our finding our voices
It led me to the obsession that was you
Is you ... will always be you
And I followed you
Followed you before you knew
I was there ... with you through the slim days
Days when there was only you
You, your Guitar y tu voz de miel
I followed
As you searched & you danced
Looking for the man you would become
Tu ... Volcán de Guatemala
I felt every Bolero
Each little twist, the Drama of every turn
In the Song of your Dance
I was listening
With ears wide open I heard you growing
I witnessed your Spirit
Locking into the explicitly sensual invitation
The irresistible drone, a Cuica impossible to ignore
The demanding, pounding pulse of the insatiable Surdo
Iyé viva meu Mes camara
Hijo de la Ceiba, I applauded your every advancement
Watched you grow as a Dancer
Watched your body become as subtle as a bowl of melted butter
I was never surprised by your greatness
Always knew you had it, that special something
And I watched
As you worked & you worked & worked & worked
You were always right in there
Serious, unbelievably dedicated, but outrageous & humorous
You might have been mesmerized by the melodic Clave of Agogo
But you were a true Artist & it was never just about the applause
The shallow glitter of Star Status never made you blind
It was the mission of the Music that kept you walking forward
Walking in integrity in a world completely out of balance
The bigger-than-life weight of your Gift ... a sacred duty
And the rhythmic voice of the Pandeiro demanded
That we heal this Planet with our love of Music & Dance

Iyé viva meu Mes camara
Aiiiii Chacho elastico
The Newspaper said that you died
I say they lied
I refused to believe it ... I could still feel you
So I followed you into the abandon of Batucada
The wildness of the Samba that you had embodied
The rhythms that had become your body were still talking to me
And again I followed you
Dove without reservation
Into the intense majesty of the obsession of your Dance
I still hear the llanto del Berimbau
Iyé viva meu Mes camara
The Press tried one more time to tell me you died
But they didn't know you & I know they lied
Hombre de goma ... I could still feel you coming on strong
You ... enduring as the bronze you colored
A gentle, but unbreakable man ... flexible as a rubber band
Iyé viva meu Mes camara
Dazed, I fell in with the traumatized crowd
And followed the call of your Song
Your impossible to ignore Tamborin
Led me all the way to the Chapel Of The Chimes
Stopped me in my tracks, threw me into a massive sadness
Crying & drenched in tears, I watched
As the drone of the Berimbau jumped up loud
And the undefeatable Spirit of Capoeira
Came down like a melodic bomb of pure unconditional love
Ran wildly, arrogantly through the crowd
Rode your Students, possessed the essence of their being
Wrapped them in the power of trance
A purely mystical gymnastic frenzy
The graceful precision of their sweaty bodies
Your legacy ... loud & proud
An undying testimony of your devotion
Your uncompromising love of the Spirit of our Ancestral Arts
Your Babies,
All but destroying the stoic cemetery silence
Slapping down the cool detachment of
Methodic Graveyard Workers
As they lowered the shell that once held you
Deep, deep down into the hungry belly of the Earth
They weren't watching the sky
They didn't see the big bird that was circling up over our heads
They didn't notice

That even the Clouds had to smile down with pride
On a job well done & wash away our fear ... our tears
How sad,
They couldn't see you as you flew away & hovered over the Grave
Dancing like a runaway Slave on the Wind
An inspiration, a force,
Creativity's never-ending discipline
What a pity ... they couldn't feel you
"Poor things" never even heard you
Laughing, that wild & crazy Carlos kind of laugh
At a Gravesite
That would never ever have a chance to hold your Soul!!!
Iyé viva meu Mes camara

SOMEBODY'S GOT TO DO IT
(WHY NOT ME?)

It's a dog-eat-dog world where the end always seems to justify the means & "more" is the only way to make it. Forget being socially, politically & spiritually correct. This is survival of the fittest! And survival of the fittest means getting "it" while the getting is good. In the end, the person who knows how to turn lemons into lemonaid will be the only person to come out on top. And on top is the place I was born to be! I'm just one of the "regular Folks" doing irregular things to make "the System" work for me. I'm no superhero & with the Planet going to hell in a hand basket as fast as it can, I know I can't save the world by myself. Took a look around, covered my nose & dove in. 'Cause the the only way to get more & put some real money in the bank was to put those unrealistic morals in my pocket & buy some of that "can't lose" Stock. I'm not going down with the Titanic & these days the wise Investor seems to be the only one who's winning. And I say, count me in!

The Stock Market is the only honest-to-God Church of the future & its Trinity is unapologetically profit, profit & more profit!!! God is green! Incarceration is a mega-billion dollar operation & business is booming. The Industrial Prison Complex is hungry & the System has a tapeworm. Survival made my decision & I'm going to get mine!

Why not??? They're closing Schools, Community Tutorial Programs gone. Recreation Centers & Youth Programs a thing of the past. Our Libraries, once neighborhood havens, stand close to extinction & the propagation of Education is considered a bad joke (a high falluting luxury) available only to snobs & "sell outs". The corner Candy Store, your Cousin's Meat Market, small Pharmacies & Family Doctors are history. No affordable Apartments for rent anywhere & no money to move even if you could. Soulful Sunday dinners, Summer "get-togethers," games on the Block & pull-out-the-stops Banquets in the Park a hallucinatory dream. You know, somebody's got to make this pay! Why not me???

Meanwhile murder & mayhem have become fashionable entertaining aphrodisiacs. (Hmmmn, sounds like an inspiring, money-making scheme for a few new Video Games.) Terror & fear have become the latest "turn on" & the cheapest & most convenient of addictive Drugs. "Mean Mugging" super Stars, psychotic-erotic Gangbangers, women-hating Pimps & sexy slasher Movies are the latest rage everywhere. Blood & guts... the adrenalin rush in The Academy Awards. Negativity glorified all over the TV, the new school craze on "Top Ten Radio" convincing Youth that violence is power & power is the only truth they'll ever need. "Bling" & "Flash" have replaced self-esteem. And these days honor is based on the price of your shoes, how much gold you wear in your mouth & how much fear you can instill. Lord......, George Orwell where are you??? (Oh well, since neither he, nor any of his disciples bothered to answer, I'm taking their silence straight to the Bank.)

In this equation of "I've got more than you," California proudly proclaims to be the home of more Jails & Prisons than a mangy dog's got fleas. We now have more of these sterile erections than any other place in the world. And greed being what greed be, they're building more. Some are calling it madness, but it simply sounds like another Business oportunity to me!

If things keep moving in the same direction, everyone will have their own personal Prison in their own backyard. A brand new low-intensity Jail on their front lawn. And if you're one of the lucky few who make it through the warfare in the streets, your Living Room may be one of those chosen to become a lucrative, private Halfway House. A Group Home where "Home Detention" is a gentler, kinder psychologically-approved attempt at "Family Reunification." A New-Age Juvenile Recycling Center, complete with the latest computer-generated programs to help your Kids relearn the Ancient Art of being Children. A creative, new, transformational concept to help them pass the time on their way to "doing Time" big-time.

I know that tongues are wagging all over town & bad mouth-ing everything I do. Let the Haters hate! There have always been those that don't want to see Folks like me with anything. But reality is, it's a win-win situation. And the icing on the cake is, you're getting "the riff raff" off the Streets & getting just what you asked for, while I'm getting richer.

I'm just a Team Player who got in on the ground floor & my investment is paying off. Everybody's safer!!! No more hoards of two-legged trash running around in the Streets. Our Streets are almost as clean as a Clorox dream & I'm fat in the pocket. Can't help it if part of the cost of the loss is most of your Families. Ain't nothing but a trade off. It may be a high price to pay, but the payoff is worth it. I've made my choice. And whether my methods are right or wrong, I think I should be thanked for helping to clean up the community. Property values are rising & my conscience is clear. I don't have any regrets & without a doubt I know deep in my heart of hearts it's absolutely worth the cost!

TIME IS A HEARTLESS BABYSITTER
(FOR BATYA, MY BABY, MY DAUGHTER, MY HEART)

Once upon a time, in a not too far away land, a land I used to know. There were still a few weird Adults around who weren't afraid to dream. A land where every Child believed that the world was full of Miracles & Magic. A world where Fairies ruled & wishes came true. An enchanting place where amusement didn't cost a cent. A world full of fun & games that most Parents didn't allow themselves to remember. It wasn't too long ago that John Henry & dancing Dragons & La Llorona were everywhere & El Cuco & Mermaids hid under the boardwalk at every beach. Brer Rabbit, Jab Jab, Wicked John & Unicorns were as common as the name of Stagolee & a game of marbles. Those were good days. Days when our Families lived in a world where the Moon followed us home & spent the night right outside our window & telephones laid eggs.

Then comes the day when Time steals the Child in our Children, erases the playful innocence of their imaginations & returns them unidentifiable. Our Kids come home devoid of any hint of enchantment. So unbelievably tainted & sophisticatedly "street wise" they rise above any memory of the good old days when mystery lived under every rock. And we come home, spitting nails. Exhausted & feeling evil from days working like dogs for unappreciative Bosses. We walk through those doors so tired & half crazy from working at Jobs we probably can no longer stand that we forget to tell the tales about the many sweet Kitchen Angels who used to sneak around sprinkling all kinds of good tasting stuff in Mama's pots.

Time is a heartless Babysitter. And gone are the days when a little tiny hug, or some fantastic tall Story would turn on the fire in our Children's smiles. Gone is the inexpensive mysterious peace of Nights when our Children felt safe, because they knew the Stars were the protective eyes of the sky. And the Sun only got up in the morning to let the Moon get some sleep & give the night sky a little time to rest. Way back in the days before Life lost its Magic & our faith in the strength of our love was the only real thing keeping us alive.

Once upon a time… In a not too far away land, a land I used to know. There were still a few weird Adults & Children around who actually liked each other & weren't afraid to have fun & dream. Not so long ago, before Time had the time to steal all the Magic & Life took the fast road & spent a lot of time running around corrupting minds & eating souls. Before the call of the street sounded sweeter than the legacy of our lullabies, gobbled up our Families, chewed them up & spit out something unrecognizable.

It was not so long ago … before we allowed Time to steal

our minds & forgot about all those good times, those happy times. Times before old wily Coyote got out-slicked by some smooth talking Microwave Mama, forgot who he was & misplaced all his tricks. Days long before we stopped looking at each other & stopped talking to each other.

And the Moon followed us all the way home & telephones laid eggs.

TWEAKIN'* & FREAKIN' IN HELL
&
EVEN THE BRIDGE LAUGHED

It was a sad, sad, sorry day when he surrendered to his worst nightmare, and the sun forgot to shine in his direction. Wife gone, children gone, house gone, job gone, pockets as empty as Mother Hubbard's cupboard! Drank up the last of the Booze, and all those good-time buddies (like all his "Good Dope") had gone "up in smoke!" These days, misery & disgust were his only real friends. Everybody else just thought he was one big joke! Even this bridge laughed at him now. Singing...

"REAL MEN DON'T COMMIT SUICIDE!
A REAL MAN DOESN'T EVEN THINK ABOUT IT!!!"

But there he was ... brand new clothes ... ringing wet with sweat ... scared to death. Just another broke & tired uppity Buppie gone down. One more Crack Monster joins the multitude of worn out "usetabe's" on the junk pile of fallen stars! Crying for what was. Crying for what could of been & what should have been. Every thing gone! Alone ... Nothing. Nothing, but a ghost of the man that was. All alone ... "tore up from the floor up". Standing on the Golden Gate Bridge looking pitiful. And this time he didn't come to listen to the seagulls sing.

He stood there. Felt like forever, looking at that bridge (as if looking at it would somehow make it go away). Depression, loneliness & guilt were his only real companions. Depression was the only thing he could depend on. And that depression & hopelessness kept him there. Kept him there looking ... waiting ... holding him in place while he tried to find some kind of nerve.

Nerve?????? What was that??? If he ever had any ... where did it go??? How could it just leave him here with nobody but a bridge & it's non-stop laughter? And like everyone else, it was laughing at him... He could almost hear it... Listen? Listen!!! Can't you hear it? It's lurking, stalking, hanging in the shadows ... whispering. Whispering in the wind ... whispering to him.

"JUST ANOTHER DRUGGED OUT JERK
TOO SCARED TO DIE, BUT EVEN MORE AFRAID TO LIVE!!!"

Every once in a while he even felt relieved knowing that it was almost over, but he was always too terrified to move. He knew it would take a whole !ot more courage than he ever had. To jump or not to jump?!?!? That is the question, the unanswerable question, or was it some kind of statement? So he just stood there … anchored by terror. Stood there … buried in terror. Stood there … frozen in an unending nightmare. Streams of nervous sweat running all down his neck … whole body soaking wet. Completely drenched in the sticky stench of his own funky sweat. Petrified by his own cowardice. Rooted like a redwood tree, unmovable as Mount Kilamanjaro. Locked in an all-out war fighting with himself & his same ole indecisiveness & the never-ending sound of this bridge's evil laughter. Blinded by tears of fear & self-hatred, he kept looking for whatever it would take to make that final jump. "This crazy shit has got to stop!" This … his curse … a wicked madness that no amount of wishing, or begging, has managed to stop! "Dammit!!! Stop!!! STOP!!!!!!" … But how??? No one would stop laughing long enough to tell him how! There was no one! There was not one person left that even gave a damn!

There had to be a way to make all the flashbacks go away, to turn back the clock & stop the world from laughing at his fall from mediocrity! There had to be a way to wipe all the smug smiles off of all those "told you so" faces! The Drugs & Alcohol had taken away everything, didn't even leave him a key to the door out of this night-mare. But he couldn't give up! He was either going to jump, or have to get off the bridge. And he was more determined than a heat wave in Hell to find the answer … had to make it all stop! He had to stop it, before it was unstoppable. He knew there had to be an answer … a way out. It had to be out there somewhere. Maybe it was sneaking around hiding in between the seagull's song & the gentle music of splashing water up against an occasional boat & the hopelessness of this suicidal nightmare & the continuous laughter of this damn bridge……. "This bridge! This damned God-awful bridge never stops & there's no way to get away from it."

"Shhhhh … Quiet! … Listen … listen. Hear it? Can't you hear???? Has the whole world gone deaf? What's wrong with everybody?" He knew there was nothing wrong with his ears. "You can hear it? … Can't you??? Listen" … It's always singing to him. "It's relentless, heartless, colder than cold, blood-curdling, whispering & signifying".

"GO ON & JUMP SUCKER!
GET OFF THIS BRIDGE & STOP WASTING MY TIME.
YOU'RE ALREADY DEAD BOY!
YOU WERE DEAD WHEN YOU GOT HERE
& YOU'VE BEEN DEAD A LONG, LONG, LONG, LONG TIME.
YOU'VE EVEN WRITTEN YOURSELF OUT OF HISTORY TRICK* MOVE OVER!
WORD IS YOU CAN'T DIE TWICE … FOOL!

STOP WHINING!

AND MAKE SOME ROOM FOR A NEW SOB STORY.
HOPEFULLY THE NEXT ONE WON'T BE QUITE AS BORING,
& HAS SOMETHING MORE THAN ONE SONG TO SING."

"Shit! It just keeps on laughing". Teasing & laughing. Making fun of all this pain & playing him like he was some kind of cat & mouse video game. Snide, salty & sarcastic! Playing him … working him. Seems like this bridge only exists to dance on his nerves. Playing him like he was only a toy … just another bad joke … playing him like his life was no big thing. Taunting & laughing & singing & laughing & whispering & laughing & singing & singing & singing…..

"REAL MEN DON'T COMMIT SUICIDE!
A REAL MAN DOESN'T EVEN THINK ABOUT IT!!!"

"SHHHHHHHH..."

THE GRANDNESS OF BLANDNESS

All I have to do is close my eyes
And I slide into memories of nights & days
When Salsa was gravy
And every one of our Musics had
Recognizably distinct personalities
Played by
Musicians who lived by the law of excellence
But then
The Son took a wrong turn
Got lost & left the Cha Cha Cha crying
The ritualistic quest for instant financial gratification
Scared the Bolero into hiding
Terrified & swimming in a bland
One-size-fits-all
Cultureless stew of corporate driven emptiness
We allowed ourselves to be force-fed
Denatured rhythm-less Hot Sauce
On passionless dance-floors devoid of heat

In musician-less ballrooms
We watched as the Mambo was kidnapped
And thrown into the same cauldron
With friends & cousins like Guaguanco & Samba
La Charanga, Danzonete, Cumbia, Festejo, Rumba,
Bomba, Merengue, Plena, Guajira, Landó & la Murga
But stone drunk on Short-sightedness, we allowed
The Gods of green paper dreams
To convince us to ecstatically self-destruct
To sacrifice the essence of our personalities
For the sake of sale-ability
Even helped to stamp out our own beautiful Cultures
And assisted our invisible partners
In the birth of a homogenized uniformity

For a few extra dollars
We gladly sold our Souls
To commodity-driven cultureless mercenaries
And got lost
In the acceptable oblivion of nothingness
Gave away our individuality
For the convenience of a dime-store reality
Leaving us with nothing

Nothing but nights dreaming of those days
Before our Cultures were homogenized
And our Salsa was still gravy

LOVE SONG FOR A LOVABLE PEOPLE

I fight so hard because I LOVE/RESPECT the EARTH
Sacred Mother of us all
Holy loving Mother raped
In the name of civilization
By those who are uncivilized, loveless, unloveable
And in "their" ugliness ..... "their" un-naturalness
"They" are jealous of your natural beauty

I fight so hard because I LOVE/RESPECT
Even the AIR I breathe/the WATER I drink
The AIR & WATER we all need to live, to love
"They" are poisoning the air, the water, our lives
"Their" unending greed is both blind & stupid
And "their" wisdom is loveless

I fight so hard because I LOVE/RESPECT CHILDREN
Happy, proud, free, healthy children
Children that dance, sing & play naked under the heavens
The #1 reason for our sweat, our love, our tears, our smiles
All our CHILDREN
Our tomorrows ..... our forevers
Our beautiful Babies forced into old age at age six
"They've" tried so hard.............
To turn our tomorrows into our enemies
Put us at each others' throats.............
That "they" might have company in "their" lovelessness
I fight to win back my Babies,
My soul, my love, my hopes, my tomorrows
Because I love

I fight so hard because I LOVE/RESPECT our MEN
My sons, my Father, my Brothers, Doctor Feelgood, my friend
You ..... Child of my belly
You ..... Son of my love
You are a physical part of me
I, Daughter of your warm sperm, born of your seed, your love
You are,
The HAPPINESS/the STRENGTH "they've" tried to castrate
"They" who would even castrate the sunshine ..... and love
You are "their" greatest fear, because it is so easy to love you
And "they" are loveless

I fight so hard because I LOVE/RESPECT our WOMEN

Woman, my Sister,
Mother of my Mother, cariñosa, preciosa, my Lover
Queen of midnight, daughter of moonlight, Love Child
You ..... Mirror of myself, strong, gentle, Cactus Lady
Lover forced to turn fighter
Queen forced to turn whore in order for us to survive
Survive "their" sickness, "their" lovelessness
"They" are jealous of your STRENGTH, your LAUGHTER
Because you are so lovable ..... and "they" are so loveless

I, created by an act of Love
Only made possible
By my wise, sensitive, strong, gentle, sensual, proud
Loving & lovable ANCESTORS
I fight so hard because I respect Love
Because I LOVE/RESPECT you, us, I, we
Because it is natural to Love
Because it is naturally respectful to love NATURE
And our natural nature that we love to love ..... each other
I fight so hard because I Love
Live for your Love
To preserve, protect & defend our Love
Among loveless people
Because I love needing you, my flesh, my blood, my people
And, because you are Love
It is impossible to do anything but love you
Live & die to love you, me, all of us
Loving us to live & dying to love you
I fight so hard because I Love
Because I love you
Because I love you, me, we, us
Because I love you
                    I love you
                         I love you
                              I love you
                                   I love you

ANCESTRAL REFLECTIONS

CALLING IN THE SPIRITS OF

ANACAONA, PAPA KÉMOKO SANO, NINA SIMONE, CORTIJO, ABDOULAYE "PAPA" CAMARA, LORD INVADER, MELBA LISTON, SABU MARTINEZ, JOHN HICKS, OLATUNJI, LINDA HILL, DON RAFAEL CEPEDA, SHIRLEY HORNE, MALONGA CASCALOURDE, EDDIE MOORE, JIM PEPPER, PEDRO JUAN PIETRI, HAZEL SCOTT, SUN RA, LUCHO GATICA, BOB BRAY, MIRIAM MAKEBA, SYVIA DEL VILLARD, FLOYD RED CROW WESTERMAN, JOY HOLLAND, PEARL PRIMUS, ELEO POMARE, ALICIA PIERCE, ARTURO SCHOMBURG, RAMITO, HORACE TAPSCOTT, ERIC DOLPHY, JAMES BALDWIN, CASPAR BANJO & ANNALEE WALKER

Can you feel them???
Ancestral suggestion trying to guide us
They're everywhere
Walking through us, right beside us
They are the essence of us
Got the intensity of their legacy in everything
All over our stuff
They're in us, with us
All the time
Our Ancestors never sleep
They want us to know all they've ever known
Been trying to show the way so we don't have to fall
They need us to feel them
Won't let us go til we let them know we need them
There's still too much work that has to be done
They've got their busy fingers in all our business
Whether we want them there or not
And they're always listening … watching … looking
Checking in on us … won't let us forget
Got to make sure their existence made a difference
Can you feel them???
They're sitting in on our everything
The Ancestors are always here … they're everywhere
Making sure we're making sure
Their influence is obvious every time we open our eyes
They need us to be aware
They gave their everything for us
They lived & died for us
They smile
Each & every time they see their lives alive in us

Feel them … they're here
Crying for us … Singing to us … Laughing at us
And right now they're dancing with us
As we carry the tradition of honoring their presence

And proudly praise & celebrate the vision they continue to give us
We humbly
Take on the mantle of the undying strength of their legacy
And pray always to be worthy of the gifts of their artistry
Can you feel them???
Insistent Ancestral suggestion on top of us, encouraging us
They're everywhere
Agitating ... trying through us to make a better way
Help us create a better day
Hardheaded, gregarious Spirits got their fingers in our everything
Relentless & instigating & they won't go away
They've been in it for the long haul
Paid the price of their tickets in commitment & blood
And they're in us ... always with us
Can you feel them???
Our Ancestors are never asleep
And we
Got to make sure their existence made a difference

GLOSSARY

Afro Beat-a popular urban music invented & popularized by Nigerian Super Star Musician, Singer, Composer & Activist Fela Ransone Kuti

Agent Orange-One of a series of herbicides used in Viet Nam. Unknown to the tens of thousands of American soldiers and Vietnamese civilians who were living, eating and bathing in a virtual omnipresent mist of the rainbow herbicides, the makers of these chemicals were well aware of their long-term toxic effects, but sought to suppress the information from the government and the public, fearing negative backlash. Of particular concern to the chemical companies was Agent Orange, which contained dioxin. Publicly, the chemical companies said dioxin occurred naturally in the environment and was not harmful to humans. Privately, they knew otherwise.

AIDS-Acquired Immune Deficiency Syndrome/SIDA

Aikido-a Japanese martial art developed by Morihei Ueshiba as a synthesis of his martial studies, philosophy, and religious beliefs. Aikido is often translated as "the Way of unifying (with) life energy" or as "the Way of harmonious spirit." Ueshiba's goal was to create an art that practitioners could use to defend themselves while also protecting their attacker from injury.

Alexander The Great-is called by many historians "a great humanitarian", but reality is that he is on record as probably having murdered more "people of color" than anyone else at the time

Anansi-A legendary deified trickster Spider (originally from Ghana).

Angel Dust-PCP, killers, matones, sherm

bad-tough, or (African American slang for...) good,

bangin'-short for gang banging, gang activity, gang membership, or I.V. drug use

Base Pipe-Crack Pipe

Berimbau-The Berimbau a Brazilian Musical obviously of African origin (probably based on the Angolan &/or Congolese bow instruments. There were no European or Indigenous Brazilians playing musical bow, while musical bows were played in both Angola & the Congo.

Bieke-nicname for the Puerto Rican Island Vieques

bochinchando-gossiping

Boricua-Puerto Rican, Borinqueño, Borincano, "Rican"

Bracero-farmworker, migrant field worker,

Bracero Laws-Laws pertaining only to Farmworkers

Buppie-a Black Yuppie

Chicano-Mexican-American

Chink-derogatory term for Chinese

Chuco-short for Pachuco

ciega-a blind woman (or ciego for blind man)

Concrete Indian-Native American who's born or lives in the city
cool-slang for: OK, wise, smart, in the know, comfortable or peaceful (see:hep/hip/deep)
Crack-rock cocaine
Crack Monster-a Crack Addict
Crank-methamphetamine, speed
Crystal Meth-"Speed" (Methamphetamine)
Cubop-Latin Jazz
Curandera-a Healer
Djali-(pronounced jolly)
dumpster diving-digging in garbage cans & dumpsters for food and/or anything else of value.
dusted-high on Angel Dust
deep-wise, smart, in the know (see:hip/hep/cool)
El Yunque-a Rainforest in Puerto Rico
51/50-crazy, not all there, insane, wacky, wack, off the hook,
Ganga-gang, el pandilla
Gang banging-Gang activity
giving five-slapping hands as a form of hand shake
Gook-derogatory term for Asians
grass-dank, marijuana
grito-shout, scream, yell, (can be used to signify pride, hello, pleasure, to announce your presence, a war cry, or pain)
Hashtar-eight string (in the Persian language of Farsi). In this case refers to a Musical Instrument made & played by living legend Ostad Mahmoud Zoufonoun
hep-wise, smart, in the know (see:hip/cool/deep)
hip-wise, smart, in the know (see:hep/cool)
Hood-short for neighborhood, see "the Hood", gangster
Hooker-Prostitute, Streetwalker, Whore
Indio-Indian (for lack of a better word the Indigenous people of the Americas were called Indians)
"in the spoon"-a person that uses heroin
Issei-1st generation Japanese-American
"Iyé viva meu Mes camara"-
Juju-African Magic
La Malinche-Native American mistress of Cortéz (a woman who's taken on almost mythic status in literature & song—sometimes as a victim & sometimes as a traitor)
La Merengona-a woman who loves to dance Mererque
La Migra-slang for Immigration Authorities
La Pachamama-Mother Earth
loaded-high on alcohol, or drugs
Los Yungas-Is a stretch of rain forest along the eastern slope of the Andes Mountains from southeastern Peru through central Bolivia. This

is the home of Bolivia's Afro Bolivian population. Yungas Road (Bolivia's Road of Death) is known as one of the world's most dangerous. This deadly 35 miles stretch between La Paz and Coroico in Bolivia is estimated to claim the lives of 200-300 travelers every year.

Mac-pimp, or hustler

Manong-A Filipino Elder

Mariachi-a Mexican Troubadour

marijuana-grass, dank

methamphetamine-Speed, Crank, Shabu

Mexarican-a slang nick name for a mixture between Mexican & Puerto Rican

Mongo-Mongo Santamaria (an award winning Afro-Cuban Percussionist)

"mule"-a low level operative who does support work for a drug dealer (such as transporting narcotics)

Nissei-2nd generation Japanese-American

Oaktown-nickname for Oakland, California

Off The Hook-crazy, 51/50, out to lunch

O.G.-slang for street Elder, Original Gangster

Operation Wetback-

Out To Lunch-crazy, 51/50, off the hook

Pachuco-A subculture of Mexican American youths during the 1940s and 1950s in the Southwestern United States. They wore distinctive clothing (such as Zoot Suits and spoke their own brand of Mexican Spanish, called Caló, Pachuquismo, or Pachuco. Being doubly marginalized because of their youth and ethnicity, there was a close association and cultural cross-pollination between Pachuco subculture & the gang subculture. A very famous Pachuco is Roy Estrada, a Bass player and former performer in the Mothers of Invention.

packin'-armed, carrying one or more weapons, strapped

pandilla-ganga, gang

pandillera-gangster, gang banger

PCP-Angel Dust, killers, matones

quo vadis-extremely close hair cut popular among African American men during the 50's & 60's

reefer-marijuana, grass, dank

Romá-Gypsies

Ruca-(Chicano slang) short for Pachuca, girlfriend

Sansei-3rd generation Japanese-American

Sabar-The Sabar is a powerful traditional Drum that comes from the West African nation of Senegal. Sabar is also a form of Music & Dance

Sarsaparilla-(*Smilax regelii)* is a trailing vine with prickly stems that is native to Central America. Known in Spanish as *zarzaparrilla*, which is derived from the words *zarza*, meaning "shrub," and *parrilla*, meaning "little grape vine." Sarsaparilla is used as the basis for a soft drink sold for its taste, frequently of the same name, or called **Sasparilla**. It is also a primary ingredient in old fashioned root beer. It's thought by Central Americans to have medicinal properties, and was a popular European treatment for syphilis when it was introduced from the New World. From 1820 to 1910, it was registered in the U.S. Pharmacopoeia as a treatment for syphilis. Modern users claim that it is effective for eczema, psoriasis, arthritis, herpes, and leprosy, along with a variety of other complaints. No peer reviewed research is available for these claims. However, there is peer reviewed research suggesting that it has anti-oxidant properties, like many other herbs.

Sassafras- Steam distillation of dried root bark produces an essential oil consisting mostly of safrole that once was extensively used as a fragrance in perfumes and soaps, food and for aromatherapy. Sassafras was a commodity prized in Europe as a cure for gonorrhea. The dried and ground leaves are used to make filé powder, a condiment served with some types of gumbo. The roots of Sassafras can be steeped to make tea and were used in the flavoring of traditional root beer until being banned for mass production by the FDA. In 1960, the FDA banned the use of sassafras oil and safrole in commercially mass produced foods & drugs. Sassafras tea was banned, until the passage of the Dietary Supplement Health & Education Act in 1994. Sassafras root extracts which do not contain safrole or in which the safrole has been removed are permissible, and are still widely used commercially in teas and root beers. Sassafras tea can also be used as an anticoagulant.

Saya-a beautiful hypnotic Afro-Bolivian form of Music

Shakuhachi-a Japanese Flute

shit-heroin, drugs, trouble, what's happening

SKAG-heroin (see:hop/in the spoon/Boy/shit)

spaced out-loaded, intoxicated, high on drugs, day dreaming, not paying attention

Speed-Crank, methamphetamine

Spic-derogatory term for Spanish speaking people

spike-hypodermic syringe

strapped-armed, carrying one or more weapons, packin'

Taiko-a traditional Japanese Drum, a dramatic Japanese artform that combines movement & percussion

The "Av"-slang for the Avenue

The Camps-in this case, the living quarters for Farmworkers

the Hood-short for neighborhood

The Joint-Prison or Jail, also can mean a marijuana cigarette

The Margin of Acceptable Risk-(Everyone I asked & every "authority" I read has a different definition. No Doctor I talked to had a definition they'd allow me to quote, but these are a few I found on the Web.)

—"The term 'acceptable risk' describes the likelihood of an event whose probability of occurrence is small, whose consequences are so slight, or whose benefits (perceived or real) are so great, that individuals or groups

in society are willing to take or be subjected to the risk that the event might occur. The concept of acceptable risk evolved partly from the realization that absolute safety is generally an unachievable goal, and that even very low exposures to certain toxic substances may confer some level of risk. The notion of virtual safety corresponding to an acceptable level of risk emerged as a risk management objective in cases where such exposures could not be completely or cost-effectively eliminated."
—"A low profit margin indicates a low margin of safety: higher risk that a decline in sales will erase profits and result in a net loss, or a negative margin."

tracks-scars made by needles
Tricks-people who buy sex, chump, fool
Tweekin'-coming down off of a "Crack" high &/or paranoia
24/7-twenty four hours a day
Vatos Locos-literally means crazy guys/Homies/guys
Vudu-(Voodoo or Voudun)-Spiritual Energy
wack-crazy, 51/50, not all there, insane
Yemaya-the Yoruba Sea Goddess

Avotcja (photo by Tom Ehrlich)

'Introducing herself as storyteller, "wild woman," a "bonafide sound junkie," who "heard Music in the rustling of newspapers in the streets /And a symphony in the sound of dripping water," nothing slows or dampens Avotcja's passion for the power and wonder of music. Guided by ancient, ancestral wisdom, she refuses to separate poetry and storytelling from song or dance. In "Blue To the Bone," her rhapsodic tribute to Oakland's uncrowned poet laureate, Reginald Lockett (1947-2008), musician-poet-broadcaster Avotcja could just as well be describing her own esthetic. "Reggie was the real deal," she croons. "No sequins, no frills, no tears, no rants / Just a one hundred percent 'Citified' Country guy / Ten steps out of the Juke Joint / And always a few seconds ahead of the Lynch Mob." The same might be said of Avotcja. Melodically keyed to what she calls "la palabra musical," Avotcja's rhythmic testament -- decades in the making – celebrates the world-changing spirit of human creativity while condemning its cold-blooded, tone-deaf assassins.'

- Al Young
- California's poet laureate emeritus

On Eliza Shefler's Drawings:

I consider myself the lucky one. Why? From the first to the last, I witnessed each image being born. Like seeds planted in a garden, they sprang to life one by one.

In these images, Eliza has shown her ability to draw in a mixture of many styles, from single line to more complex, detailed drawings. In this group of works, Eliza has captured the spirit of this powerful, one of a kind book.

With the publication and release of this book, I am very excited to see Eliza get the chance to show her work to a wider audience.

Anthony J. Smith
Commissioned Sculptor, Painter, Singer/Songwriter